# ASTOUNDED

ENCOUNTERING *GOD*
IN EVERYDAY MOMENTS

## ANGELA DONADIO

BRIDGE
LOGOS

Newberry, FL 32669

**Bridge-Logos**
Newberry, FL 32669

**Astounded:**
**Encountering God in Everyday Moments**
by Angela Donadio

Copyright © 2020 by Bridge-Logos

Revised First Edition

Printed in the United States of America.

Library of Congress Catalog Card Number: 2020939772

International Standard Book Number: 978-1-61036-253-5

Cover Photo:
Amber Trementozzi, AMT Photography | amtphotography.smugmug.com

Makeup:
Melissa Eadie, Melly Beauty Makeup Artistry | www.melissaeadie.com

Clothing:
Tiffany Lupo, LuLaRoe Tiffany Lupo | lularoetiffanylupo@gmail.com

Cover/interior design:
Kent Jensen, Knail LLC | knail.com

All biblical quotations unless otherwise noted are from the New International Version (NIV): Scripture taken from The Holy Bible, New International Version ®. Copyright © 1973, 1978, 1984, 2011 by Biblica, Inc. Used by permission of Zondervan.

## DEDICATION

To Dale, my husband and partner for life. Thank you for the way you love me and encourage me to follow God's call on my life. To Gabrielle and Christian, my children and now, my friends. Thank you for cheering me on and loving me through every adventure. To every woman who holds this book in your hands, I pray you encounter God in everyday moments and start living astounded.

# TABLE OF CONTENTS

# FOREWORD

Dear Reader,

Oh, how I wish that I knew your name! I would love to address this letter to you personally because I deeply desire to communicate heart-to-heart with you as you ponder whether or not this book is for you.

So, would you promise to do something for me? Would you promise to take a pen, cross out the word "reader" and place your own name in that place? You see, I yearn to have a sweet connection with you as I write this foreword for my dear friend, Angela Donadio.

Angela is a woman that I am watching ... I am watching her life with grand anticipation of all that she will become. She carries an anointing and an ability to communicate truth with her life that is uncommon. We need more Angela Donadio's in our world today. She is not afraid to take a stand based upon Scripture and has embraced unyielding faith in spite of a culture gone wild.

In many ways, Angela and I are the same person although we are separated by about 15 years of life. Let me share with you what Angela and I have in common:

- *We both love the Word of God so much that it fills nearly every sentence that comes out of our mouths.*
- *We are both pianists.*
- *We are both married to pastors and leaders in the Body of Christ.*
- *We were both raised in homes of deep faith.*
- *We both love being moms!*
- *We have both laid down our lives for the cause of Christ.*

However, there is one component to Angela's personality that is startlingly different than mine – she is an adventurer and I am not. I love a cup of tea by a roaring fire with a good book in my hand … Angela loves to climb mountains, to sleep in tents on foreign soil and to ride ridiculous roller coasters. I'll pray for her while she rafts down white waters and snorkels in critter-infested waters from the safety of my back porch!

Angela's spirit of adventure and her zest for life are communicated on every page of this book. You will fall in love with Angela as she takes you on a journey through the life that she loves and how she has met Jesus in dentists' offices, in the aftermath of car accidents and while watching a Hallmark movie. Angela is "every woman" but she is more than that. Angela is a girl who is head over heels in love with Jesus and is determined to wring the joy out of the life she has been given.

Angela's heart of purpose and promise is clearly observed on every page of this devotional. She has held nothing back as she invites you to live a life of astounded faith and of astonishing hope.

If you are looking for a devotional that is filled with zest yet lasting truth, you will love Astounded!

If you want a devotional that you can share with your daughters and with your mother, then Astounded is the devotional for you.

If you simply want more of Jesus in a lasting way, you will find Him on the pages of Astounded and in the heart of Angela Donadio.

Blessings, my friend—

CAROL MCLEOD, Best-Selling Author and Speaker
Author of *Significant; StormProof; Guide, Guard, Grace*; and *Vibrant*
www.carolmcleodministries.com

## ACKNOWLEDGEMENTS

Thank you, Jesus. You know me better than anyone else and love me best. Thank you, Dale. Your love steadies me through every adventure. I love doing life with you. None of this would be the same without you. Thank you, Gabrielle and Christian. You've taken this journey with me and I'm forever grateful. No matter what happens in life, keep your compass pointed north to Jesus. Thank you, Mom and Dad. You invested your time, energy, love, resources, and most of all—Jesus—into my life. Watching you weather life's challenges framed the way I view my own. Thank you, Mom Donadio for proofing this manuscript and walking down memory lane with me.

Thank you to my extended family and family in heaven. Thank you, River of Life Church for over 25 extraordinary years of ministry.

Thank you to those who graciously extended your endorsement of this book. I admire your leadership and unwavering faith more than you'll ever know. Thank you, Suzanne Kuhn and the Brookstone Creative Group for your support and representation. Thank you, Suzi Wooldridge and the Bridge Logos Family. I've loved every moment of these three projects together!

# ENDORSEMENTS

The first story I heard Angela share was about her Mount Kilimanjaro climbing journey. She told about the disappointment of not being able to summit the mountain (AFTER A YEAR OF TRAINING), and as she spoke, she connected in a profound way to me and her audience. *Astounded: Encountering God in Everyday Moments*, does the same thing. It is rooted in honesty and reflection—an encouraging narrative of daily life struggles and the joyful realization that God is walking with you in each moment. Angela fills each page with transparency and hope—as she did the first time I heard her share a story.

LISA POTTER, Executive Director of Women Who Lead,
Potomac Ministry Network

---

I love how Angela hits everyday situations, struggles, and successes head on in her *Astounded: Encountering God in Everyday Moments* devotional. Bringing a practical approach to finding miracles in ordinary moments, Angela helps you discover purpose in the mundane as well as the miraculous through her personal touch while pointing you to Jesus. You will leave each day encouraged with practical steps to live your best life, have a renewed outlook, and unearth God in places you never knew you could. It's a daily breath of fresh air you will want to read over and over, and one you will want to share with others.

JESSIE SENECA, Founder of More of Him Ministries,
Author, Speaker, and Leadership Trainer

I rarely enjoy inspirational devotional style books yet *Astounded* is one most-welcome exception. Instead of the usual light-weight faith fluff, Angela Donadio provides some deep, soul-searching considerations through her candid personal stories—stories of our jointly shared human realities that we don't readily admit. Beyond inspiring us to consider our ways, Angela offers clear and compelling direction for us to embrace the higher ways available to us as new creatures in Christ. Angela's heart to see women become all God intended is evident as this book is clearly a passionate investment in her mission. This is the one book of this type, I wholly recommend.

REV. PAMELA CHRISTIAN, Award-winning Author of the *Faith to Live By* series, Speaker, Media Personality, International Evangelist and Apostle

Angela's stories ripple with authenticity and promise of a life lived on purpose. Through vulnerability and humor, she points out all the quiet places we find God working in our ordinary lives, and she encourages us to sit at his feet in worship, to conform to his image, and to proclaim his astonishing mercies to the world around us. These devotionals will deliver accessible doses of heaven into your day. Enjoy!

SUE SCHLESMAN, Author of *Soulspeak: Praying God into Unexpected Places* (Selah Award finalist 2019)

Angela has a beautiful writing style that keeps the reader engaged by skillfully weaving timeless Bible truths together with unique and compelling real-life experiences. With encouraging devotions to meditate on weekly, I highly recommend *Astounded* as your next devotional!

DONNA SPARKS, Author & Assemblies of God Evangelist

Prepare to feel loved and cherished!! *Astounded* is a constant reminder of how God is in every moment of your every day. Each devotional will have you feeling refreshed and renewed as Angela lives out loud and walks you through extraordinary challenges with a truly loving God.

*"Those who look to the Lord their faces will be radiant"*

PSALM 34:5

JANET SWINK, Fellow Sojourner and BFF for 25 years

---

Have you ever felt worn out from disappointment? Exhausted from the repeat cycle of releasing your burdens to Jesus only to pick them back up again? You are not alone. In *Astounded*, Angela shares raw and vulnerable truths of her own disappointments and how God astounded her in the most unexpected and painful circumstances. Using biblical application and personal reflection, Angela challenges us to experience the power of viewing our daily life through a holy lens. Her devotional teaches us that a surrendered heart is the catalyst for seeing extraordinary miracles in our everyday lives.

KIM BOHN, Brain Tumor Thriver and
Founder/Owner of Beaded Miracles

#LIVEASTOUNDED

# SOUL CONDITIONER

*"He parted the heavens and came down...He reached down from on high and took hold of me; He drew me out of deep waters...He rescued me because He has delighted in me."*   PSALM 18:16-19

*"Ouch! That hurts!"* Eyes scrunched and fists clenched, I fought the urge to reach up and grab the comb from my mother's hands. Removing the tangles from my long, blonde hair was unavoidable. But, when I was the one holding the comb for *my* young daughter, I was so thankful for conditioner!

Unfortunately, our hair isn't the only thing that needs detangling. Disappointment, loss, and relational conflict can leave knots in our hearts. The root of conflict is unmet expectations. Part of taking care of our souls is learning to release unrealistic or unmet expectations of others and ourselves and trust God as our Source. In Psalm 18, David describes the dangers of finding ourselves tangled up in life.

God asked Samuel to anoint David to succeed Saul as the King of Israel. However, he waited years to assume the throne. The time between the anointing and appointing proved agonizingly difficult. God's hand on David enraged Saul, who still held the position. Eaten alive by jealousy, Saul hunted David and his rag-tag army of 600 men through desert caves and strongholds. David penned the words of this Psalm as he learned to trust God as his Protector. Psalm 18:4 reads,

> *"The cords of death entangled me; the torrents of destruction overwhelmed me."*

*Wow.* David was in serious need of soul conditioner. We may not find ourselves hiding out in a cave, but we often retreat to hiding places in times of trouble. Sometimes, we look to protect ourselves through counterfeit sources of security. We wall our hearts and guard our emotions. We bury our pain under never-ending piles of work. We mask our problems through unhealthy attachments and addictions. Yet, David discovered the secret passageway out of trouble:

> *"I called to the Lord, I cried to my God for help."*

God always longs for us to call to Him, but especially in times of turmoil. I absolutely love God's response:

> *"He parted the heavens and came down...He reached down from on high and took hold of me; He drew me out of deep waters...He rescued me because He has delighted in me."*

He conditions our soul with peace and detangles the knots in our hearts. These three principles and prayers strengthen us during those seasons.

**Patience.** Be patient with yourself and others during the process. Anything worth having takes time. Resist the temptation to become frustrated when progress seems slower than you'd like. We can rest in the promise that God works with us and on us to perfect His image and character in our lives.

*Prayer: "God, what do you want me to learn through this?"*

**Persistence.** Don't give up when you find yourself between the anointing and the appointing. His call on our life develops in cooperation with our obedience. Trust God to fulfill His will, His way.

*Prayer: "What is one step I can take today?"*

**Perspective.** Seek God's heart for the knots in your own. A damp, dark cave seems an unlikely place to encounter the presence of God. Yet, God used an unfair and unjust situation to bring about promotion in David's life. Ask Him to give you an eternal view on a temporary circumstance.

*Prayer: "God, how can you receive glory from this?"*

David's obedience was not in vain, and neither is yours. He became King, and God called him a man after His own heart. Look at the conclusion of Psalm 18 in Verse 46:

*"The Lord lives! Praise be to my Rock! Exalted be God my Savior! He is the God who avenges me, who subdues nations under me, who saves me from my enemies. You exalted me above my foes; from a violent man you rescued me. Therefore, I will praise you, Lord, among the nations; I will sing the praises of your name."*

Our loving heavenly Father can untangle any knot. I can't promise it won't hurt a little, but when He is finished, your soul will thank you.

**Astounded,**

*Angela*

# PRACTICE THE GRACE ERASE

*"One who loves a pure heart and who speaks with grace will have the king for a friend."* PROVERBS 22:11

Before the days smart phones recorded our every move, a lovely couple in our church invited us over for dinner. About 6:45 p.m., our house phone rang.

*"Hey Dale. Just checking to see if you guys are on your way over for dinner?"*

My husband and I stared at each other incredulously. Both of us had completely forgotten to make a note of the date. Considering we were sitting on the couch in our sweats having finished dinner at home, yeah, you can surmise the rest. We stood them up. Our mistake cost that precious couple time and money and could've cost us our relationship with them had they not been so gracious. Years later, now we laugh with them about the debacle.

Mistakes happen. *A lot.* Sometimes, we are at fault. And other times, someone else is to blame for an error that costs us resources, time, or energy. When we make a mistake, our instinct is to panic, get defensive, or even lie to hide the mistake. Perhaps you've been there...

You wake up to a dead car battery and realize you didn't turn off the lights. You get called into the boss's office to explain why the books aren't adding up properly. You completely forgot to send that email you promised and now everything is delayed.

Or, perhaps you've been on the other side of a mistake, where someone's negligence, irresponsibility or lack of knowledge costs *you* something...

You make it all the way home from picking up dinner only to realize you were given the wrong order. You leave work early for an appointment only to find out they rescheduled you and forgot to leave you a message. You spend countless hours finishing a project because your team members fumbled along the way...

Mistakes can cost us in lost productivity, money, and time. They can also cost us mental and emotional frustration. Just to clarify, I'm not talking about colossal mistakes that belong in the category of sin. That's a conversation for another day. I'm talking about honest mistakes that could have been avoided had someone been more aware or responsible. The kind of mistakes where we want to give someone a piece of our mind and let them know just how much added stress they caused us. Yeah, those mistakes. So how can we handle mistakes with grace?

## PRACTICE THE GRACE ERASE BY RUBBING MISTAKES OUT INSTEAD OF RUBBING THEM IN

**When we're the ones making mistakes:** Be honest. Don't lie, hide or deflect blame. Admit responsibility and validate the other person's feelings. "I'm sorry" goes a long way.

Be open. Mistakes serve as a teacher. Receive correction as an investment into your life.

**When we're on the receiving end of mistakes:** Be honest. Yeah, we can't really get around that either way. Share your feelings in a constructive way. Frame statements from an "I perspective" instead of "you did..." and focus on what can be mined out of the rubble of a mistake.

Let it go. We can't control our emotions, but we can control what we do with them. Acknowledge emotion without allowing it to find a stronghold and drain your reserves. Usually, the person didn't intend to cause you frustration or pain.

Mistakes require grace. Next time someone stands you up for dinner (can you tell I'm not sure I'm over it?), forgive them and put another date on the calendar. Next time your spouse irritates you because they forgot to do something they promised, talk it over calmly and come up with solutions. Next time your child exasperates you because their mistake cost you extra work or finances, try rubbing the mistake out instead of rubbing it in. After all, aren't we thankful God originated the grace erase? Whew. I sure am.

**Astounded,**

*Angela*

# THE POINT IN DISAPPOINTMENT

*"And hope does not disappoint, because God's love has been poured out into our hearts through the Holy Spirit, who has been given to us."*
ROMANS 5:5

Out of the corner of my eye, I catch the familiar sight of his worn-out blue tennis shoes. He kicks dirt my way and my stomach knots.

*"Not again,"* I whimper silently. *"Can't I get through a single recess without this mean kid ruining my day?"*

*"What's the matter? Ya scared?"* he bellows.

Gripped with fear, I don't dare turn around. *"Just act like you don't hear him and maybe he'll go away,"* I try to convince myself. Just then, the end-of-recess school bell screeches over the loudspeaker, and I exhale at the welcome sound. Startled and emboldened, I turn on my heels to stare him straight in the face.

*"You're just a big ol' bully, Timmy Marshall."*

And—at least for today—I make it through recess, unscathed.

Some seasons in life feel like one long recess, ruined by the school-yard bully of emotions: disappointment. One simple sentence can knock the wind right out of us, taking with it our hope.

*"You didn't get the job."*

*"There's nothing more we can do."*

*"You can't have children."*

**Disappointment is deflated hope.** Behind every disappointment is an unmet expectation. The school-yard bully of emotions preys on our hope, paralyzing us with fear and intimidation. After a few tough rounds with disappointment, I realized I was facing each new day "guard up, hopes down."

Perhaps you can relate. Something doesn't turn out at all like we hoped, and we feel the sting of discouragement. We know God has a plan for our lives; we just didn't think it would look like this. But what if we stopped looking at disappointment as a bully and started seeing it as a friend? I reframed disappointment after some serious soul-searching and honest prayer. It changed the way I viewed the bully I had come to loathe. We can make disappointment work for us when we see that *God* is at work for us.

## WHAT IS THE POINT IN DISAPPOINTMENT? DISAPPOINTMENT BECOMES A FRIEND WHEN WE SEE IT AS A SIGN THAT POINTS TO...

**God's Instruction.** Disappointment points to places we have misplaced expectations. God wants us to place our hope fully in Him. In Exodus 5, Moses expressed his frustration that despite his obedience, God's people remained in slavery. Rather than look to Pharaoh for deliverance, God wanted Moses to trust in Him.

In the following chapters, God gives Moses clear instructions that change the course of Israel's destiny. God listened to Moses, and He listens to us. In the safety of God's presence, mourn your disappointment, release your expectations, and listen for His instruction. *The point: Where have I placed my hope?*

**God's Protection.** Disappointment points to places God protected us from things that weren't His will. We can unwittingly hope for something that God never intended. A closed door may be God's providential protection. Throughout Paul's missionary journeys, God closed doors not as a sign of rejection, but as a sign of protection. Begin to thank God for ways He protected you from things that could have hurt you far worse than the sting of disappointment. *The point: What is God trying to protect me from?*

**God's Redirection.** Disappointment points to places God wants to move us in a different direction. The book of Ruth shares the story of a woman who lost her husband and moved to a foreign country with her bitter mother-in-law. She could never have imagined the blessing on the other side of brokenness. Don't become stuck in the bitterness of disappointment. Embrace redirection as a sign of God's favor. *The point: In what way do I need God to redirect my life?*

We don't have to lose the battle with the school-yard bully of emotions. We can live "guard down, hopes up" when we see the point in disappointment. Ask God to help you reframe disappointment and inflate your hope.

"*Ya scared?*" Disappointment hollers.

"*Nah,*" we answer with a grin. "*I get the point.*"

**Astounded,**
*Angela*

# PINT-SIZED FAITH

*"May the God of hope fill you with all joy and peace as you trust in him, so that you may overflow with hope by the power of the Holy Spirit."* ROMANS 15:13

One summer, our family spent two glorious weeks resting and refreshing on the beaches of the South Carolina coast. On the last day, while sitting peacefully in my green lounger, umbrella overhead and intriguing book in hand, a little girl stole my attention. Her squeals of delight filled the ocean air, captivating my heart. She could not have been more than five years old. I watched as this blonde-haired girl attempted to tackle the waves licking the shore. Placing her fingers securely around her pint-sized board, she ventured into the ocean, a few more feet each time, armed only with the hope of riding in on a wave.

Several joyous minutes passed before Mom, Dad and baby brother waded into the ocean to join her. Distracted by Mom's fabulous bubble-gum pink swimsuit, it took me a minute to notice that unlike his sister, the little boy wanted nothing to do with the waves. I observed as Dad patiently encouraged him to try to catch one. The teary son was unable to be persuaded and was gently passed to Mom's waiting arms. Dad turned his focus to his daughter and picked her up briskly.

Against the expansive horizon and endless sea, she seemed nothing more than a doll. Hands on her waist, he carried her out to meet wave after crashing wave as she held firmly to her board. She was giddy with expectation as Dad walked her well past the places where she could swim on her own. *"Fearless,"* I thought to myself. Dad waited until the time was right before turning toward the shoreline. With a giant shove, he pushed her onto the crest of the oncoming wave. She was flying, and for a moment, I was too. Transformed by my imagination, her plastic board became a colorful, tapestried magic carpet, soaring over salted sea.

*"Do it again, Daddy!"*

I marveled as this beautiful father-daughter dance repeated again and again until the ocean's playground wore her out. Her body may have been tired, but her spirit was undaunted. The magic carpet received a much-deserved rest as father and daughter walked triumphantly back to shore.

Safe in her father's arms, board firmly in hand, this brave girl painted a stunning portrait of faith. Yes, on my own, I can enjoy the refreshing but shallow waters along the sand. Trusting in my Heavenly Father's strong arms, however, I allow Him to pick me up, Bible in hand, and carry me much farther than I would ever dare to go alone. Prompted by His timing and propelled by His grace, I ride the wind of the Spirit in ways I never could have dreamed.

Romans 15:13 shares,

*"May the God of hope fill you with all joy and peace as you trust in him, so that you may overflow with hope by the power of the Holy Spirit."*

As we place our confidence in the God to perfect anything that concerns us, we experience the reward of trust. He fills us with joy and peace through the power of the Holy Spirit. Instead of feeling flooded by worry, we overflow with hope.

We are so tempted to place our hope in so many things. People. Bank accounts. Promotions. A different spouse. A healthier body. But if we tether our trust to anything but God, we will be sorely disappointed. Instead, faith trusts God to make a way. Where do you need God to move in your situation? We can release anything into His capable hands. Whatever you may feel anxious about today, remember God has the final say in your situation. God understands those moments when it's all we can do to wrap our cautious fingers around our pint-size faith. Allow God to pick you up. He makes us brave.

*"Do it again, Daddy!"* We can trust our Father to carry us into deeper waters, stronger waves, and a more exhilarating ride with Him.

**Astounded,**
*Angela*

# SILENCE
# SELFISHNESS

*"Aha, the gate of the peoples is broken; it has swung open to me. I shall be replenished, now that she is laid waste."* EZEKIEL 26:2

Growing up, the sound of 88 keys on a piano and voices in three-part harmony often filled our home. Not surprisingly, a love for music compelled me to pursue it as a career. I can't imagine my life without the joy of leading worship, or writing a song, or simply listening to a beautiful melody. My heart halted for a moment as I read Ezekiel 26:13,

*"And I will stop the music of your songs, and the sound of your lyres shall be heard no more."*

Tyre, a highly cultured city, famed for its exquisite music as it reverberated off the Mediterranean Sea, sat silent.

Ezekiel's prophecy in Chapter 26 depicts utter destruction of the notorious city whose name meant "rock." Once renowned for strength and wealth, the shock of battering rams beat down her walls. Horses and chariots trampled through her streets as dust billowed into the air. Riches became plunder and men, women, and children became casualties of war. Fishermen dried their nets on her scraped soil once covered by the merchant princes.

Splendor laid bare. Significance stripped. Purpose obliterated. Why? What was their crime?

The secret lies in Ezekiel 26:2.

*"Aha, the gate of the peoples is broken; it has swung open to me. I shall be replenished, now that she is laid waste."*

As Tyre watched God's people suffer judgement, they rejoiced at the opportunity to take advantage of Jerusalem's demise. Their proximity as prominent cities made them financial rivals. Seeing Jerusalem as a commercial competitor, Tyre welcomed her collapse as their gain. Yet, although Jerusalem was under divine judgement, that was not an excuse for other countries to celebrate her punishment. God is a just Judge; He cannot look aside. Eventually, Tyre was completely decimated, a sobering illustration of the danger of selfishness.

Selfishness distorts our perspective, causing us to view someone else's trial through a lens of "how this might benefit me." *Their bankrupt business could increase my bottom line. Their failed marriage might make mine look better. They got what they deserved; now maybe there is more room for me at the table.*

We grieve the heart of God when we celebrate someone's struggle. Selfishness shoves its way to the front. Selflessness makes space for others. Selfishness looks for the opportunity at someone else's expense. Selflessness looks for the opportunity to expend itself for others.

## SELFISHNESS SILENCES OUR PURPOSE— SELFLESSNESS RESPONDS WITH GRACE

I'm ashamed of times in my life where I let selfishness guide my choices. When feelings of inadequacy rear their ugly head, I resort to measuring my worth against someone else's success or struggle. We fall into a dangerous trap when we try and push open opportunities instead of letting God move His way. I feel most vulnerable when I think there might not be enough room for me at the table. In those moments, I lean into the reminder that He is my Provider. This helps me take my eyes off myself and on to the needs of others.

Selfishness is rooted in a scarcity mindset, driven by the false belief that one person's pain is another's gain. We can silence selfishness. As we selflessly yield ourselves to God, we trust that God *is* and *has* enough for me. We don't need someone else to fail in order to succeed. Instead, we can choose to let God use us as instruments of peace as we help others recover their purpose.

**Astounded,**
*Angela*

# WHEN A PAIR OF SHOES MAKES ALL THE DIFFERENCE

*"Stand firm then, with the belt of truth buckled around your waist, with the breastplate of righteousness in place, and with your feet fitted with the readiness that comes from the gospel of peace."*

EPHESIANS 6:14

*"What's the point of having surgery if my knee still feels this bad?",* I grumbled to my husband.

A year after surgery to repair a torn meniscus in my knee, physical therapy, and a couple of cortisone shots, my knee still hurt. Like, hurt hurt. It kept me up at night and prevented me from wearing anything but flats. (I know, horror of horrors.) It hindered my ability to stand for more than a few minutes without pain. The prospect of losing my ability to exercise altogether loomed over me like a dark cloud. Before I resigned myself to give up something that brings me joy and relieves stress, I explored every remaining option. A trip to an alternative doctor offered little comfort.

Hence, the grumbling to my husband. Sitting on the couch to nurse my knee and a crummy attitude, something on social media caught my eye. A friend, an avid runner, complained about her sore knees.

*"Yeah, I feel your pain, sister,"* I instantly mused.

Then her next sentence changed it all: *"I just got a new pair of running shoes and I'm not in any more pain!"*

*"Are you kidding me?"* I sat, stunned. *"After all this, maybe I just need a new pair of shoes?"*

You'd think painful arches and burning shins would've given me a clue. But I was looking in all the wrong places for a solution to my problem. I headed to the local athletic store where they carefully watched my gait and suggested several pairs for my specific needs. I pulled on the teal and purple cross-trainers and the heavens opened. Okay, maybe not literally, but it was a world of difference. Within just a few days, my knee didn't hurt. Like, *at all.* I actually wore heels. Come on y'all. To take heels from an ex-pageant girl is like taking candy from a baby. Who knew a pair of shoes could make such a difference?

As I tightened my laces to head to the gym, I felt the gentle voice of the Holy Spirit. *"Angela, I'm glad your new tennis shoes are alleviating your knee pain. I'm pleased you discovered a solution to the problem. But what shoes are you wearing?"* Now, I know God cares about the number of hairs on my head, but I didn't really think He was talking about my tennis shoes or my olive-green wedge heels. Nope. I knew what he meant.

Ephesians Chapter 6 shares the wardrobe that equips us with spiritual strength for our daily battles. Paul describes the full armor of God this way:

> "Stand firm then, with the belt of truth buckled around your waist, with the breastplate of righteousness in place, and with your feet fitted with the readiness that comes from the gospel of peace. In addition to all this, take up the shield of faith, with which you can extinguish all the flaming arrows of the evil one. Take the helmet of salvation and the sword of the Spirit which is the word of God. And pray in the Spirit on all occasions with all kinds of prayers and requests."

Truth be told, during that season, my feet were not fitted with the readiness that comes from the gospel of peace. The tragic death of our longtime family dog, a contentious political climate, and a swamped schedule rendered me spiritually dry. I conceded my peace to shoes of doubt...anger...excuses. Peace requires us to pause through prayer and release built-up frustration. **Peace comes when I get close enough to God's heart to settle my own.**

Paul connects the message of the gospel to the shielding and supportive footgear of the Roman soldier. When we wear God's one-of-a-kind shoes, we're protected by peace. Maybe you're nursing a painful situation right now. A new pair of cross trainers might do the trick for an aching knee, but only the peace of God provides the remedy for a burdened soul. Let God's peace clothe you as you press in close enough to His heart to settle your own.

**Astounded,**
*Angela*

# THE COST OF A PENNY

*"Don't you know that a little yeast leavens the whole batch of dough? Get rid of the old yeast, so that you may be a new unleavened batch—as you really are."*  1 CORINTHIANS 5:6-7

It actually costs more to *make* a penny than it's worth. Why is this on my mind, you ask? I learned the cost of a penny the hard way. Some of you may remember the days when cars came furnished with round cigarette lighters that glowed fire-engine red and burned an uncountable number of fingertips. Alas, with the dawn of smart phones, companies repurposed those sockets as phone chargers. Having successfully dated myself, I'll move on.

I reached to plug my phone into the car charger, only to find a penny firmly lodged in the round base. My husband managed to get it unstuck and I proceeded to charge my phone. *Nothing.* Thinking that was odd, I tried my daughter's charger with the same result. *Nothing.* Now, I don't know much about electronics or the effects of metal on metal, but somehow that penny short-circuited the whole thing.

I put off taking my car into the shop for repairs, instead grabbing my home charger every time I walked out the door. I paused constantly throughout my day to plug in my phone in the most inconvenient of places. On days I forgot my charger, I limped through without phone or text access. Nowadays, we purchase multiple chargers for every possible home and remote location. Which leads to another point altogether; we are far too dependent on our phones. But I digress.

I never even noticed the tiny penny had snuck into my car charger until the damage was done. Often, I toss them carelessly on the ground. Yet, something so seemingly insignificant added frustration to my daily schedule and caused costly repairs. The whole thing got me wondering about how often we let sin creep into our lives and lodge in uninvited spaces. And when we do, what is the cost? Paul taught on this very subject in 1 Corinthians 5:6-7.

*"Don't you know that a little yeast leavens the whole batch of dough? Get rid of the old yeast, so that you may be a new unleavened batch—as you really are."*

His analogy warns of the dangers of tolerating sin, even in small doses.

My father-in-law, Patrick Donadio, was a gun-wielding gang member until Jesus radically saved him from himself. He knew firsthand the cost of sin and the power of grace. Shot by the police during a burglary, he spent subsequent time in jail before he surrendered his life to the Lord and served as a missionary and Christian leader his entire life. Before his promotion to heaven in 2012, he often mentioned this quote from an unknown author in his sermons: *"Sin will take you further than you want to go, keep you longer than you want to stay and cost you more than you want to pay."* We must be ruthless with sin. We can't allow it to, like that pesky penny, find a home in us. Unaddressed, sin has the potential to rob us of the abundant life God planned and promised. Sin always has a cost, no matter how small. The little white lie...the hidden purchase...the extra glance, burrow like parasites into the landscape of our soul.

Here's the great news: you don't even need to spend a penny for the gift of God's grace. He freely offers forgiveness for any sin through salvation in Jesus Christ. Simply ask Him to be your Savior, confess your sins, and receive His forgiveness. You will start on a journey to becoming new in Him. That, my friend, is *priceless*.

Perhaps the penny will always find value in the hands of a four-year-old child standing on their tiptoes to throw it— and a wish—into a fountain. Lodged among other pennies and wishes, it finds a home. The lesson I learned from a penny gave it renewed value for me, too. The next time you hold one in your hand, let it remind you of the cost of sin—and the power of God's amazing grace.

**Astounded,**

*Angela*

# NEVER GO OUT
# OF STYLE

*"Has no one returned to give praise to God except this foreigner?"*

LUKE 17:18

*"Is it 1985?"* my husband asked with a grin. A telling glance at my black, fuzzy leg warmers clued me in on the reason for his snide comment.

*"No, thank you very much. These are totally back in style. I should've kept the ones I wore in high school,"* I quipped back. We had a good laugh over throwbacks that return for a second chance. For the record, I'm all about the reappearance of leg warmers, but I sure hope 6-inch bangs and mullets stay firmly planted in the past.

If you wait long enough, a retro fad will be cool again. Whether you're wearing a pencil skirt or bell bottoms, one thing never goes out of style: saying, *"thank you."* I surveyed a group on social media to find out what type of *"thank you"* made them feel most valued. When offered the choice between a text, email, phone call or handwritten note, most preferred opening a thank you card from the mailbox. Phone calls and face-to-face conversations landed a close second. Some didn't care what form; they just appreciated being thanked!

Call me old-fashioned, but I love writing and receiving handwritten notes. A decorative box holds a stack of some of the favorite ones I've received throughout the years. I peruse back through them from time to time. When life is busy making withdrawals, saying *"thank you"* makes deposits. For me, reading thoughtful sentiments never goes out of style.

**Gratitude matters to Jesus.** Perhaps nowhere is this more evident in Scripture than in a story found in Luke Chapter 17. While traveling through a village, ten men afflicted with leprosy stood at a distance and called out loudly, *"Jesus, Master, have pity on us!"* Miraculously, He healed all ten.

Yet, perhaps even more incredulous is what happened in Verse 15:

> *"One of them, when he saw he was healed, came back, praising God in a loud voice. He threw himself at Jesus' feet and thanked him—and he was a Samaritan. Jesus asked, "Were not all ten cleansed? Where are the other nine? Has no one returned to give praise to God except this foreigner?" Then he said to him, "Rise and go; your faith has made you well."*

Healed of a horrid disease that rendered these men utter outcasts, one returned to thank Jesus. *Only one.* The man's praise is even more profound to Jesus considering the deep-seeded tension that existed between the Samaritans and the Jews. Jesus never let man-made barriers keep Him from divine appointments. He recognized the man for his heart of thanksgiving and honored him for his faith. This story may have occurred 2000 years ago, but the message is just as relevant today.

## CONSIDER IMPLEMENTING THESE SIMPLE TIPS TO EXPRESS GRATITUDE

Keep a stash of birthday, sympathy, and encouragement cards on hand, or lower your costs by making your own notes with card stock and a sharpie. Text yourself a reminder to send out a thank-you card after a dinner in someone's home, a graduation gift, or *"just because"* they deposit into your life.

Mail a thank-you note within two weeks of an event. At a minimum, send a gracious text or email within 24 hours. Keep a running list of addresses for friends and family on your computer or in a vintage address book. Yep, they still exist. Check out online sources that send free personalized cards for any occasion. Use social media to publicly thank someone. How different our world would be if our timelines were filled with deposits of gratitude instead of withdrawals of gripes.

Our everyday moments become trends worth remembering when we make the deposit of gratitude. Let's watch for ways to say *"thank you"* to our spouses, our kids' teachers, our cashiers, and our friends. More than anything, let's live the kind of life someone else wants to thank. You don't have to be up on the latest fashion to be in style. Rock those leg warmers. Just don't forget to say, *"thanks."*

**Astounded,**

*Angela*

# THE TRUTH IN RED LETTERS

*"But Jesus often withdrew to lonely places and prayed."*

LUKE 5:16

*"Why would a church put that on their digital sign? On a main road, no less,"* I thought to myself, slightly offended. In glaring, red, all capital letters, flashed the jarring question: **"IS PRAYER A WASTE OF TIME?"**

*"Of course, it's not! Why even ask that question!"* I exclaimed aloud in my car. My neck craned backwards to read it again, as if in slow motion. My thoughts became deliberate and the moment grew heavy. I contemplated, *"Is prayer a waste of time?"*

I wanted to instantly dismiss the question as a blatant attempt to garner curiosity. I wanted to bellow a resounding, *"No!"* to the query. I wanted to retort with a mountain of evidence, piled high from my stacks of recent prayers. But honesty began to bleed onto the page of my well-wishes. If truth be told, my prayer life was little lackluster. Okay, maybe a *lot* lackluster. I could rattle off excuses. Yet, there, in flashing neon lights, was the truth.

I want to make my case for the importance of prayer. Yet often, my actions betray me. If I really believe in the power of prayer, why don't I live what I believe? Could I, *gasp*, harbor the dangerous notion that prayer is a waste of time? I know, beyond a shadow of a doubt, that prayer changes things and prayer changes people. Prayer is our lifeline, our means of communicating with God. Prayer repositions our heart and refocuses our attitudes. Prayer energizes our spirit and gives us renewed purpose. Prayer allows us to hear the heart of our Father for our life and the lives of those we love. Prayer gives us God's perspective and provides divine solutions.

See, I can make my case for the importance of prayer. But if all of that is true, and I know it is, why isn't it my highest priority? *Maybe it's because I think I can figure things out on my own. Maybe it's because I think my time is better spent doing something else. Maybe it's because I don't think my prayer is really making a difference.* Whatever the reason, and maybe it's all of the above and more, change begins by being honest. It's painful to acknowledge that I needed those audacious red letters. I needed a wake-up call. I needed the reminder that *I can't figure things out on my own... that my time is best spent in prayer...and my prayers really do make a difference.*

I mulled that sign over a hundred times. I asked God to forgive me for the times doubt or self-reliance crowd out my reliance on Him. After all, prayer is admitting I am wholeheartedly dependent on God. **Prayer should be our first defense, not**

**our last resort.** If Jesus valued prayer, how much more should we? Luke Chapter 5:16 shares,

> *"But Jesus often withdrew to lonely places and prayed."*

- He prayed for His disciples, that their faith would not fail.
- He prayed in the Garden, that His will would line up with the will of His Father.
- He prayed on the Cross, asking His Father to forgive those who were crucifying Him.
- And now? He prays for us.

The enemy wants us to feel condemned when we're faced with the reality of a dull prayer life. Stay encouraged through the promise of Romans 8:34.

> *"Who then is the one who condemns? No one. Christ Jesus who died—more than that, who was raised to life—is at the right hand of God and is also interceding for us."*

Jesus knew I would see the truth in red letters that fateful day. And, He prayed I would feel *determined* rather than discouraged. The starting point to anything meaningful is prayer. Perhaps difficulty has dampened your prayer life or pride has kept you from admitting your dependency on God. Take heart; Jesus is praying for you. And that, dear friend, is the truth.

**Astounded,**
*Angela*

# A LIFE-SIZE SCREEN PROTECTOR

*"So Shadrach, Meshach and Abednego came out of the fire, and the satraps, prefects, governors and royal advisers crowded around them. They saw that the fire had not harmed their bodies, nor was a hair of their heads singed; their robes were not scorched, and there was no smell of fire on them."*     DANIEL 3:26-27

I've lost it. Dropped it. Left it on top of my car. Drenched it from the incoming tide. And, horror of horrors, heated it up in the microwave in place of my coffee. My poor abused phone. I've certainly earned my spot in the phone "Hall of Shame." I don't mean to be cruel to my phone; it's just a dreadful combination of distraction and downright negligence. During an overextended season, I picked up my phone to discover a huge crack across the entire width of the screen.

*"What in the world?"* I said out loud. *"When did this happen?"* It wasn't until the next morning that I had the nerve to tell my husband, Dale. (The previous phone fiasco resulted in Dale braving icy rain for two hours to search for my missing phone on the side of the road after I left it on top of my car. Ahem.)

*"Honey, I cracked my phone. I have no idea how I did it!"* My son picked it up and validated my fear. *"Yep, Dad, it's really bad."*

*"I don't understand!"* I protested. *"I even bought a great case and a screen protector! I paid an extra $10 and the sales lady guaranteed me it would keep my phone from cracking! It's not supposed to be able to crack!"*

**Insert my "a-ha" moment.** *A screen protector.*

*"Wait! Christian, can you get the sheet protector off and see if maybe it's just the protector that's cracked?"* I asked with palpable optimism. And sure enough, we peeled back the damaged, cracked, pitiful screen protector to find the phone perfectly intact. Insert giant sigh of relief, and my second "a-ha" moment. This ordinary moment became an opportunity for God to download an extraordinary truth.

Friends, life happens. We get dinged, cracked, bruised, and bumped. Some of us traveled the lonesome path of my phone; feeling lost, overlooked, or washed up with the tide. Some days, we look as though we, too, got inadvertently short circuited in a microwave. Most of us would pay *far* more than a few bucks for a life-size screen protector. Yet, God offers it for free; we simply need to put it on. When we place our trust in an unfailing God, we're covered with His protection. Trials and temptations attempt to weaken our resolve and get us to crack under pressure. But faith in God's heart protects our own.

In Daniel Chapter 3, we meet three Hebrew young men taken as captives to Babylon. King Nebuchadnezzar ordered a statue built in his honor, 90 feet high and 9 feet wide. He commanded nations far and wide to bow down and worship his image. When word came to the King that Shadrach, Meshach and Abednego, devout Jews, refused to obey, he was incensed and threatened to throw them into a fiery furnace. Their response stunned the King:

> *"King Nebuchadnezzar, we do not need to defend ourselves before you in this matter. If we are thrown into the blazing furnace, the God we serve is able to deliver us from it, and he will deliver us from Your Majesty's hand. But even if he does not, we want you to know, Your Majesty, that we will not serve your gods or worship the image of gold you have set up."* DANIEL 3:16-19

They bound the three men and threw them to their death. Yet, to King Nebuchadnezzar's amazement, a fourth man stood in the fire: Jesus. Because of their bold faith, God covered them with miraculous protection; not even a hair of their head was singed. In Daniel 3:28, we see the incredible result of their deliverance in the words of the King:

> *"They trusted in him and defied the king's command and were willing to give up their lives rather than serve or worship any god except their own God."*

He issued a decree requiring all nations to worship the one, true God: Jehovah.

That challenging workplace? God's got you covered.

That overwhelming problem? God's got you covered.

That cracked relationship? God's got you covered.

The precious blood of Jesus stands as our defense and protects us from the enemy's targeted attacks. No matter what you face, God's got you covered.

**Astounded,**

*Angela*

# A TRAIN WORTH CATCHING

*"We demolish arguments and every pretension that sets itself up against the knowledge of God and we take captive every thought and make it obedient to Christ."*   2 CORINTHIANS 10:5

I reached a conclusion after a visit to New York City with my daughter and some friends: there is no easy way to get around this place.

You can walk, which we did, for *miles*. My feet had the blisters to prove it. You can take a taxi, which we did once, prompted by said blisters. You can drive, which we did, but it included a myriad of tolls, an inadvertent run through the E-Z Pass Lane, and a hefty parking ticket outside our hotel for misreading a sign. Yeah, ouch.

Or, you can take the subway train. It became our primary mode of transportation, and prompted spirited conversation such as:

*"What train are we supposed to be on? L? E? Q, R, S, T, U, V...???"*

*"Are we headed Uptown or Downtown?"*

*"Could it be any hotter underground?"*

And most importantly: *"Hurry up and get in before the train shuts its doors!"*

I was terrified that one of our group would get left behind on that subway platform, miss the train, and lose their way. That got me thinking. Far too often, I allow my train of thought to leave me stranded while it heads off to destinations like "Fear," "What if?" and "Not good enough." Perhaps, like me, you could use some encouragement to *"catch that train before you lose your mind."* The Bible has a *lot* to say about how and where we travel with our minds.

What we choose to meditate on, or think about, will determine our words, and ultimately, our behaviors. If you'll pay close attention to the words that come out of your mouth, you'll discover a lot about your thought life. Our words reveal areas we tend to struggle in such insecurity, fear, jealousy, or pride. They also disclose a deficiency in gratitude or mercy. However, we can't just change our words; we need to change the underlining root system behind them. Thoughts dictate behaviors and actions. Every destructive behavior can be traced back to a faulty thought pattern—a false belief. The enemy combats our minds with lies about God, ourselves, and others.

You may have walked through life with the belief that you have no control over your thought life. That simply is not true. The Holy Spirit can sanctify, or set apart, our thought life and make it holy and pleasing to the Lord. We aren't merely victims of an unmanageable thought life; we have choices about what occupies our minds. We can't always control when a thought knocks on the door of our mind, but we don't have to give it a home. Paul understood the influence of our thought life, and wrote about it in 2 Corinthians 10:5.

> *"We demolish arguments and every pretension that sets itself up against the knowledge of God and we take captive every thought and make it obedient to Christ."*

**What are we supposed to take captive? Our thoughts. What are we supposed to do with them? Make them obedient to Christ.**

*Doubt knocks.* Don't give it a home.

*Insecurity knocks.* Don't give it a home.

*Temptation knocks.* Don't give it a home.

The thoughts we allow to take up residence in our mind will determine our beliefs, actions, and our destinies. Don't let your train of thought run away from you and cause you to lose your way. Instead, make every thought obedient to Christ. No matter where you travel this week, whether by taxi, car, or train, keep in mind that God is with you—*and for you*—in your everyday struggles. That's a train worth catching.

**Astounded,**

*Angela*

# NOWHERE TO GO BUT UP

*"Come up here, and I will show you what must take place after this."*
JOHN 4:1

I am not a morning person. Rolling out of bed while it is still eerily dark constitutes a small miracle. Nonetheless, while in Phoenix, Arizona for a women's conference, I was highly motivated to set my alarm for—yawn—4 o'clock in the morning. The night before, I had spotted a brochure in the hotel lobby advertising a glorious way to experience the Sonoran Desert. I couldn't resist the opportunity to do something I had dreamed about for two decades. With the lure of freshly brewed coffee and the promise of adventure, I managed to persuade a dear friend to join me. Throwing caution and common sense to the wind, we headed out, a la Thelma and Louise, to enjoy an exhilarating ride aboard a hot air balloon.

We arrived at the launch site to discover our brightly colored balloon stretched out over the desert floor. After giving us a few safety tips, our guides began inflating it using large tanks filled with propane. I have to admit, it was at this moment I wondered if a thin sheet of nylon, shooting flames of fire, and a small wicker basket seemed a wise combination, especially considering it was about to be my mode of transportation. *"You only live once,"* I thought to myself. I awkwardly threw my leg over the rim and climbed in.

We lifted off and took flight, propelled only by fire and wind. Within moments, golden and auburn hues filled the Arizona sky as the sun majestically broke over the mountain ridge. It had been a long time since I had watched a sunrise. Too long. Loosely directed by our fearless pilot, we began steadily ascending to 1200 feet until we were soaring in the open air. Everything looked different. I *felt* different. I breathed deeply, acutely aware of the silence and serenity I had been missing back on the ground. Flying high above cactus and circumstances, I received an unexpected gift: a transformed perspective.

In Revelation Chapter 4, we find John, Jesus' beloved disciple and the author of the Book of Revelation, on the island of Patmos. Exiled in a state of incarceration, he literally had nowhere to go but up. On an island of isolation, Jesus extended an invitation: *"Come up higher."*

*"After this I looked, and there before me was a door standing open in heaven. And the voice I had first heard speaking to me like a trumpet said, 'Come up here, and I will show you what must take place after this.' At once I was in the Spirit, and there before me was a throne in heaven with someone sitting on it. And the one who sat there had the appearance of jasper and ruby. A rainbow that shone like an emerald encircled the throne. Surrounding*

*the throne were twenty-four other thrones and seated on them were twenty-four elders. They were dressed in white and had crowns of gold on their heads. From the throne came flashes of lightning, rumblings, and peals of thunder. In front of the throne, seven lamps were blazing. These are the seven spirits of God. Also, in front of the throne there was what looked like a sea of glass, clear as crystal. In the center, around the throne, were four living creatures, and they were covered with eyes, in front and in back. The first living creature was like a lion, the second was like an ox, the third had a face like a man, the fourth was like a flying eagle. Each of the four living creatures had six wings and was covered with eyes all around, even under its wings. Day and night, they never stop saying: 'Holy, holy, holy is the Lord God Almighty,' who was, and is, and is to come."*

Limited by his surroundings, John experienced the unlimited presence of God. We, too, are invited to come up higher; to walk through the door of worship. You may feel isolated on an island of circumstance. Perhaps it seems there is nowhere to go but up. When we get a fresh revelation of who God is, we receive the gift of perspective. If the fear of heights, or just plain sanity, scratches a hot air balloon ride off your list, not to worry. Simply take Jesus' hand and *"Come up higher."*

**Astounded,**
*Angela*

# *MY SINKING DECK*

*"Therefore, everyone who hears these words of mine and puts them into practice is like a wise man who built his house on the rock."*

MATTHEW 7:24

The first sounds I hear nearly every morning are the spirited conversations between the birds that make my back yard their home. One season, however, their lovely melodies were drowned out by the deafening buzz of power saws. The culprit? A sinking deck. When we first built our home, we had a deck built on the back of the house. After about ten years, I observed a slight slant to the left when I stepped outside my back door. With each passing month, I noticed the slant became *not* so slight, requiring that I step down and not just out. A board began to bow, then another board, followed by nail pops and a distinct downward slope. The inevitable was happening: our deck was sinking.

What began as a small annoyance turned into a full-blown safety and stability issue. My husband called in expert carpenters from our church to determine what caused it and what needed to be done. They carefully examined the floor of the deck, pushed on warped boards, and climbed underneath for a closer look. We faced a two-fold diagnosis: the deck had not been properly bolted to the house to begin with, and the foundation had not been built up with backfill to compensate for water runoff.

The solution? Tear up the entire deck floor, jack up the deck, backfill the land, and anchor it to the house. *Sigh.* When the project was underway, I walked outside one morning to bring the guys a pitcher of ice water. We began to discuss the spiritual lessons our sinking deck provided. First, it's a recipe for disaster to build anything without a proper foundation. Additionally, you must have a strong anchor. It took ten years to manifest, but a problem we couldn't see—more than ten feet down—eventually made its way to our door.

So it is with our spiritual walk. Our lives must be built on the strong foundation of the Word of God and firmly anchored to Jesus Christ. We need to deal with sin and issues that no one can see *before* we begin to sink. In Matthew 7, Jesus shares this analogy:

> *"Therefore, everyone who hears these words of mine and puts them into practice is like a wise man who built his house on the rock. The rain came down, the streams rose, and the winds blew and beat against that house; yet it did not fall, because it had its foundation on the rock. But everyone who hears these words of mine and does not put them into practice is like a foolish man who built his house on sand. The rain came down, the streams rose, and the winds blew and beat against that house, and it fell with a great crash."*

In this parable, Jesus contrasts the actions of the wise and foolish builders. The wise builder is one who hears the words of Jesus and puts them into practice. He experiences rain, wind, and storms, yet the foundation stands because it was built on the rock. The foolish builder is one who hears the words of Jesus but does nothing with them. He also experiences rain, wind, and storms, but his house fell because it was built on sand. Both hunkered down to brave the same bad weather, but only one stood strong. Although we aren't promised a trouble-free life, we don't have to sink. Take time to lay a solid foundation. It might cost you a little more in time and discipline, but *not* doing it will prove far more expensive.

The morning our deck was complete, I awoke once again to the birds' sweet serenade. As I stepped outside onto a new, level deck, I thanked God for His Word as the foundation of my life. Trials will come. Storms will rage. But, when we are anchored in Jesus, we will stand.

**Astounded,**

*Angela*

# THE CRUEL, HORRIBLE WRESTLING MAT

*"We are pressed on every side by troubles but not crushed and broken. We are perplexed because we don't know why things happen as they do, but we don't give up and quit. We are hunted down but God never abandons us. We get knocked down, but we get up again and keep going."*  2 CORINTHIANS 4:8-9

The anxiety started long before I pulled into the school parking lot. As much as I wanted to support my son in all his endeavors, I absolutely *dreaded* junior-high wrestling matches. I'm the one who encouraged him to follow in his dad's footsteps as a State-Champion wrestler. That was before I went to a match. Let me share a flashback from my first experience.

My heart rate rises the moment my middle-aged backside finds a middle-school bleacher to call home for an hour plus of sheer torture. A sea of purple emerges from the locker room, and

I scan the nervous and expectant faces to find my son. In the split second our eyes connect; after all, God forbid, a middle school child wave at his half-crazed mother in the stands. I'm instantly taken back to a more innocent time when the day's priority was to keep my rambunctious toddler from skinning his knee. A rush of heat floods my face as I realize that the second my son decided to put on a singlet, we crossed a rite of passage. I become keenly aware that despite my best efforts, I will not be able to protect him from pain in this life.

The referee steps onto the mat and the match begins. The *cruel, horrible wrestling mat.* I guess it really isn't the mat's fault. It just lays there, dashing their hopes before their six-minute match is finished. I watch as each boy fights with every ounce of his being to avoid one thing: being pinned to the mat.

I'm far too unnerved to stay seated like a normal mom. Instead, I find myself pacing and screaming wildly from the sidelines. I wince, bury my face, and even turn around as boys contort their bodies into unimaginable shapes. They stretch shoulder ligaments nearly, and sometimes completely, past their limits. The mat holds the promise of victory or the taste of defeat. The difference between the two? *About an inch.* That's all that separates a boy from being pinned, once an opponent has him on his back. I watch as many, including my son, exhaust all possible options to keep the last corner of his shoulder off the floor. The referee is down on both knees, eye level with the mat, and optimism lives until his hand slams against the mat. Pinned.

During what proved to be our only wrestling season, (thank God), I would constantly yell to his team: *"Go to your base! Stand up! Ten more seconds! You can hold him off! Keep your shoulder up! Fight!"*

**And it hits me: life is that mat.** Illness, bruised relationships, and the demands of ministry threatened to pin me. I've held the hand of my sisters in Christ as they faced their own formidable opponent.

A young first-time mom loses a baby at five months.

A woman's happily ever after turns into a nightmare beneath the dark cloud of infidelity and broken trust.

A widow searches for peace and purpose after sudden tragedy.

The inch between our shoulder and the mat is a powerful space. The enemy pronounces himself referee and waits at eye level to slam his hand and yell triumphantly, *"This one is pinned."*

## BUT GOD

We have more than a thin singlet, flimsy headgear, and gold shoes that convince a 14-year-old boy he will have a better chance of gripping the mat. As we follow our Heavenly Father's footsteps, we stay undefeated. Jesus is our Master Coach, knowing just the right instruction to give at just the right moment. The Holy Spirit never sits on the sidelines. Within us, He is our Guide, Comforter, Teacher and Encourager.

We won't escape the wrestling matches of life. But we have the power to overcome and keep that last vestige of shoulder off the mat. Remember Paul's words in 2 Corinthians 4:9.

*"God never abandons us. We get knocked down, but we get up again and keep going."*

And that noise you hear? That's just me, running along the sidelines, cheering you on to victory.

**Astounded,**
*Angela*

# TURN AGGRAVATION INTO OPPORTUNITY

*"Do to others as you would have them do to you."*     LUKE 6:31

Bad attitude in tow, I steadied myself for the dual pain of dental impressions and payment for treatment to remedy issues with my jaw. However, before I even sat down in the doctor's chair, we hit a snag. Prepared with my bank account and routing number from my savings account, the accountant let me know the funds had to be automatically withdrawn from a *checking* account. After 15 minutes of haggling over a solution, I lifted my cell phone to flushed cheeks and called my husband, Dale.

*"I don't know what to do but this account won't work for automatic withdrawal,"* I said with a twinge of irritation.

*"I'm almost to the bank. Let me run in and see what we need to do."*

30 minutes later, my jaw sore from probing and impressions complete, Dale called back.

*"It's all squared away. They switched accounts, but they didn't know why the doctor's office couldn't just take it. They said that's never happened before. Call me back when you're done."*

It wasn't until I left the office that I realized the unnecessary aggravation was a set-up for divine opportunity.

Dale began to tell me what happened in the bank that we've used for years. The manager knows us well. In the middle of the business transaction, her voice quivered.

*"Dale, can I ask you a personal question?"*

*"Sure."*

She hesitated. *"If you don't like somebody, are you going to go to hell?"*

My husband adjusted from patron mode to pastor mode. *"Well, I don't think so but...is there anything you want to talk about?"*

*"No... I just don't know why bad things happen to good people and bad people continue to get away with things. I don't want to start crying."*

She shifted back to business until she couldn't hold back her tears.

*"My mom passed away last week, and this is my first day back."*

He offered his sincere condolences and identified with her ache, having lost his dad just a few years ago. As she shared, her pain became palpable.

*"My niece is not making good choices, and now I'm raising the child she had out of wedlock. She just keeps on being irresponsible, and she's pregnant again. Why would God allow my mom—a good, loving mom—to die unexpectedly of cancer, and yet allow this mom to go on acting the way she is?"*

Dale continued to talk to her, ministering to her broken heart. They finished the business matter and she wiped her tears.

*"Dale Donadio, you were just supposed to come to this bank today. This shouldn't have even happened—that company should've been able*

*to take funds out of either account. But I needed to hear what you had to say."*

And that, ladies and gentlemen, is what you call a divine appointment. Sometimes we get so frustrated with unnecessary aggravation that we miss the opportunity to bring healing and hope.

## HOW DO WE TURN AGGRAVATION INTO OPPORTUNITY?

**Listen.** Dale was barely three weeks out of knee replacement surgery. Yet he chose to be fully present, and actively engage. It's amazing what God can do with us when we slow down and listen.

**Empathize.** Stay dependent on the Holy Spirit, following His cue to enter into someone else's pain. Dale shared some of his own emotions during a difficult season of his life, letting her know that she wasn't alone in her struggle. Empathy is powerful; use it lavishly.

**Ask.** Most people want to unburden their heart, and many are open to prayer. Dale asked open-ended questions and let her control the direction and pace of the conversation.

The next time aggravation begins to boil over, look for the divine set-up. Stay open to a possibility that you didn't see at first glance. It might just be opportunity knocking.

**Astounded,**

*Angela*

# GOD'S MAKEOVER MIRACLE

*"Let perseverance finish its work so that you may be mature and complete, not lacking anything."*  JAMES 1:4

It all started with my red couch; my once unique, now obnoxious couch. I might also mention that 13 years of lounging and entertaining took its toll on the value-priced sofa. After several nights of, *"My back hurts sitting on this couch...this couch gets on my nerves...I'm tired of all this red...,"* my husband consented to look for a new one.

However, the more I thought about it, it wasn't just the couch we needed to replace. All that surrounded it begged for transformation. What began with one piece of furniture evolved into a makeover of the entire main floor. I know, I know, my husband is a saint. We trekked laps around Lowe's and scrolled through hundreds of paint swatches. It soon became evident that my quest for a new living room sectional entailed a few hiccups.

In my naiveté, I hoped the whole downstairs floor could be painted in a week while we traveled for spring break. But, when the painter came to give an estimate, we realized the enormous amount of prep work necessary before he could even *begin* to paint. He sanded away color block designs. He puttied over dents. He patched over scrapes. He repaired things I hadn't even seen until he pointed them out to me.

*"I know you're really anxious to change everything, but you don't want me to start painting yet,"* he explained. *"If I paint over these designs and stripes, you'll see them under the fresh coat of paint. Plus, every ding and nick will show. You don't want me to rush the process. You can't paint over a hole."*

His words were still hanging in the air when I felt the gentle voice of the Holy Spirit. *"You can't paint over a hole."* I began to ponder how often I wished God would speed up the process of maturity in my life. I'm impatient when I'm yearning for change. I'm too quick to ask God to slap a fresh coat of paint over an area that requires the thorough process of renovation. He knows the toll life takes on my heart, tenderly revealing the prep work I desperately need. He sees the bumps and scrapes that only His grace can fix. He observes the dings that demand the putty of a new perspective. He painstakingly smooths rough, damaged areas as I wait in His presence. He applies the fresh coat of change as I spend time in His Word. **Transformation requires renovation**.

My home was a complete mess during that makeover season. We covered furniture in plastic and shoved it to the center of rooms. We stripped beloved artwork from walls and prepped them for paint. With each space unfinished, I felt undone. Yet, we persevered, and eventually, the beauty of the completed process emerged. Holes were patched. In fact, you would never even know they were there. Every step of the makeover was worth it.

Perhaps you're feeling the wear and tear of life. Maybe unresolved family problems put a dent in your joy, or unfulfilled dreams left a mark on the walls of your heart. If we want to experience God's makeover miracle, we can't paint over a hole. James 1:4 encourages us to let the process of perseverance finish its work, so we will be mature and complete, not lacking anything. If the process of perseverance is left undone, *we* are left undone. Too often, we fight the process when we don't see the promise.

Think of perseverance as the gold mined out of a trial or test. God allows our faith to be tested because He knows it is the only way to develop perseverance and character. He is more interested in our character than our comfort. Invite Him to take a close look at any area that needs His touch. When you feel tempted to ask God to hurry, allow Him, instead, to have His way. Don't give up when it seems like it's too big of a challenge. The process might take a little longer than we would like, but the miracle makeover will be worth it. Don't get discouraged when moments are messy. When our lives are in God's hands, the transformation is spectacular.

**Astounded,**
*Angela*

# HOPE FOR THE REST OF US

*"Your word is a lamp for my feet, a light on my path."*

PSALM 119:105

The Bible is everything we could ever need, anytime we need it. An emotionally charged Psalm. An edge-of-your-seat Old Testament story. A challenging New Testament letter written from a seasoned pastor. A glimpse into the footprints of Jesus through the Gospels. Hope. Peace. Encouragement. Instruction. Guidance. Provision. Strength. Protection. Insight. It's all there... all in one place: *The Bible*. In a pinch, I'll pull it up on my phone, but there's nothing like the feel of the sacred pages of Scripture between my fingers. Yet, despite all the Bible promises, some days it sits unopened.

You know those days; the ones when *"something, someone, some errand, some activity, something I won't even remember in twenty-four-hours"* became more important than reading the living Word of God. It hurts to type it, but it's the truth. Perhaps you can relate to the old, *"Let me open my Bible and wherever my finger lands is God's heart for me today,"* kind of Bible reading? Yeah, I've had those moments, too.

We are just so overextended. Some of us have littles under our feet 12 hours a day and struggle to get a shower. Some of us work 12 hours a day and struggle to find time to spend with those littles. We take care of aging parents, shuttle pre-teens to a myriad of activities, and battle health issues that drain our energy. I get it, I really do. **But an unopened Bible is a sign of an overextended life.**

We can do better than this. Surely, there is a better way. Meet Mama Azuka. I met this barely-5-foot tall, soft spoken, Nigerian Bible teacher, on one of my trips to Kenya. She packed so much knowledge of the Word and dynamite into her tiny frame, I had to know her secret. She shared without reservation: for decades, she purposed to dedicate a "10% tithe of her time" to God every day. Yep, you read that right. That's *two hours and forty minutes a day* she spends in prayer and study. I want to be Mama Azuka when I grow up.

However, she didn't start there. She started small; ten minutes a day...twenty minutes a day...an hour a day... until she fell so in love with Jesus that the *"someone, something, some errand, some activity, something I won't even remember in twenty-four-hours"* were not more important than Him. To top it all off, she oozed compassion for those of us who struggle to find our 1%. Aware we needed a better approach than the whole "eyes-closed-random-finger-pointing-thing," she imparted a massive dose of wisdom and six questions that change the way you read the Bible. I left Kenya awash with hope for rest of us 1%-ers.

## IF YOUR UNOPENED BIBLE REVEALS AN OVEREXTENDED LIFE, IMPLEMENT THIS STUDY METHOD INTO YOUR QUIET TIME

Select anywhere between ten verses to one chapter of the Bible to read each day. Then, use these six questions to amplify and apply the passage. Put the questions on a notecard or type them into your favorite smart device and turn any space into sacred ground.

What is this passage saying about God? (Is there something God wants me to know about Him?)

What is this passage saying about me? (Is there something God wants me to know about me?)

Is there a sin I need to confess? (repent, ask forgiveness, renounce)

Is there a command I need to obey?

Is there a promise I can claim?

Is there an example I need to follow?

Then, ask the Holy Spirit to narrow your focus to one or two verses that express His heart for you. Write it down or text it to yourself to read throughout the day. That's it! We can do this, right? Come on, 1%-ers. This week, we will just say *"no to that someone, something monster,"* and dust off the best Friend, wisest Counselor and greatest Encourager we'll ever meet: The Bible. Mama Azuka, *our overextended souls thank you.*

**Astounded,**

*Angela*

# FIVE WAYS TO ACHIEVE LESS AND DISCOVER MORE

*"Come to me, all you who are weary and burdened, and I will give you rest. Take my yoke upon you and learn from me, for I am gentle and humble in heart, and you will find rest for your souls. For my yoke is easy and my burden is light."*

MATTHEW 11:28-30

I'm such a do-er. Anybody relate? One of my life-long pursuits included ridding myself of the yoke of perfection. Perfection is relentless. Never satisfied, it continually places unattainable demands on its prey. For an over-achiever, that constitutes cruel and unusual punishment. Thankfully, God offers a much better way. He invites us to come to Him and receive His rest.

No matter how we're wired, many of us struggle with the discipline of rest. Rest is recalibrating. Rest is healing. Rest is an invitation to reset the strained sinews of our soul. As we embrace rest, we make peace with the sacred space of less. Those holy moments refit our hearts with God's custom-made yoke. He beckons us to achieve less of what is holding us back from His best so we can discover more of His purpose and plan. Then our *doing* is grounded in our *being* in Him.

## HERE ARE FIVE WAYS TO ACHIEVE LESS AND DISCOVER MORE

**Worry less, pray more.** Pray when worry threatens your peace and discover more joy. Worry is a negative form of prayer. Reframe your worries by turning them into petitions and prayers to an ever-present God who wants to carry your burdens for you.

**Do less, pause more.** Pause when a plethora of invitations place unrealistic expectations on your shoulders and discover more purpose with intentional choices. Turn your focus to being more than doing. Seek to be present, compassionate, and wise, and you'll lay a healthy foundation for what you decide to do with your time, resources, and emotional reserves.

**Stress less, purge more.** Purge areas of mental, emotional, and physical clutter and discover more clarity and bandwidth. Entertaining negative thought patterns and self-talk is not only destructive, it's incredibly draining. Redirect negative thoughts through the filter of Scripture and replace them with what God says about you and your situation. Let go of unforgiveness and doubt and embrace grace and trust in a loving Heavenly Father. Organize areas of physical clutter that breed anxiety. You only have so much space, energy, and time. Choose quality over quantity and notice less stress and increased margin in your life.

**Complain less, practice gratitude more.** Practice gratitude when discontent rears its ugly head and discover a healthier perspective on life. It takes more energy to complain than it does to respond to your surroundings with positivity. Life doesn't always play nice. But complaining only cements a bad attitude by rehearsing the worst possible outcomes. Look for ways to become more thankful and patient with yourself and others.

**Rush less, pace yourself more.** Pace yourself and discover more time for who and what really matters. Rushing is a sign of an overwhelmed schedule and an undisciplined life. Learn to listen to your body's alarm bells: headaches, fatigue, tight shoulders and elevated blood pressure. Spot signals from others that indicate they're feeling slighted or unimportant by your tight schedule. Slow down and savor moments. Eat slowly. Read a book slowly. Breathe slowly. Your heart will thank you in more ways than one.

Longing to encounter God in new ways? Allow Him to reset the rhythm of your life. Take it from a recovered perfectionist—that custom-made yoke looks good on you.

**Astounded,**

*Angela*

# A MUZZLE-FREE ZONE

*"Set a guard over my mouth, Lord; keep watch over the door of my lips."*
                                                            PSALM 141:3

I love dogs, and we've owned several: Sophie and Scarlett, our pugs, Snowball, a Shi-Tzu, and Chewie, named for Chewbacca, our current Shih-Tzu, and the most spoiled member of the family. Chewie healed our hearts after we lost Snowball at the age of 12 in a tragic accident. When we called the groomer to line up Chewie's first appointment, they braced for the worst. After all, Snowball was a biter. He never bit us, but goodness sakes, he was protective and thought he was a pit bull in a toy dog's body. He was a member of our family for so long, I thought it only fitting to include one story about Snowball that still resonates today.

*"Hello, Mr. Donadio?"* The voice on the other end of the phone quivered with anxiety. *"I see that Snowball is on my schedule*

today for grooming. Ummm, were you able to pick up the sedative we talked about?"

"Yes, I sure did," my husband responded, managing to hide our embarrassment. After all, what dog needs a sedative to get his hair cut and groomed? Our dog, that's who. He was terrified of grooming and groomers were terrified of him. We gave up two times and rescheduled with the promise of a sedative.

"Well," the shaky voice continued. "Are you aware that sometimes a sedative makes a dog more aggressive?"

Great, my husband thought. Just what we need; ramp up the intensity on an unmanageable dog in desperate need of a haircut.

"No, I didn't know that."

"Yeah, it can happen sometimes. Do you by chance have a....muzzle? Or could you go buy one before you come and stay with him?"

My husband obliged and braced for the unpleasant task ahead with dog, sedative, and muzzle in hand. Cranky from a sedative, unsettled by the groomer and frazzled by a muzzle, which covered his entire head, poor thing, Snowball did his best to derail the haircut. An hour later, my husband was covered in dog hair and Doggy-Owner shame.

I never understood why Snowball hated haircuts so much. Chewie loves them. I wholeheartedly look forward to an hour of pampering every few weeks, thank you very much. But I can understand why he hated the muzzle. Why is it so hard to muzzle our mouths? I'm far more likely to raise my voice when I'm tired, impatient, afraid, or hurt. Whatever our reasons, it's no excuse for an un-muzzled mouth. We sin with our mouth through gossip, complaints, a critical spirit, crude language, or just down-right nastiness. It's pretty difficult to praise God and encourage others with a mouth full of venom. Our words are an overflow of our hearts. When I deal with my heart issues, my mouth follows.

We create a muzzle-free zone when we saturate our hearts with God's Word. The Bible has a *lot* to say about this topic.

In Ecclesiastes 5, Solomon counsels us not to allow our mouths to lead us into sin. James tells us if we can control our mouths, we can keep our entire body in check. In Ephesians 4, Paul encourages us to only let out of our mouths what is helpful to building others up according to their needs. When we're focused on the needs of others, we're far less likely to wound them with our words. If you want to create a muzzle-free zone with your life, pray the words of Psalm 141:3.

*"Set a guard over my mouth, Lord; keep watch over the door of my lips."*

Even though our groomer winced when she saw Snowball's name on her schedule, she mourned with us over our loss. Snowball reminds me, not only of countless family memories, but to guard my life so no one has to wince from my words. He grew up alongside my children, traveled with my husband to work, and brightened our vacations. God wants to use our lives, and our words, to bring hope and healing into overheated places. Use your voice to shine a light on injustice...to speak up for the oppressed...to comfort the broken-hearted...to sow life into those you love.

**Astounded,**
*Angela*

# WHEN YOUR WANT-TO IS WORN OUT

*"When Jesus saw him lying there and learned that he had been in this condition for a long time, he asked him, "Do you want to get well?"*
JOHN 5:6

It's downright embarrassing to disclose the lengths I went to recently to get seen by a dentist. A tooth that clamored for consideration soon demanded my full attention. I put off my unease of the dentist chair until I couldn't stand the discomfort another minute. Pain is a powerful motivator, and I finally gave in. I was desperate.

X-rays confirmed my suspicions: a tooth with a 20-year-old root canal deteriorated beyond repair, requiring antibiotics and a visit to an oral surgeon. It wasn't the news I hoped to hear, but I wanted to do whatever it took to get well. I'll confess; I'll drive to

Timbuktu for a doctor when I'm in excruciating pain, but I don't always pursue God's prescription to treat matters of the heart. I know He *can* do it, I'm just not sure I *want* to. Sometimes I'm flat-out stubborn, and sometimes I'm flat-out worn out.

When we nurse damaged relationships or screaming emotions, we tend to ignore things that need attention because it's too painful. If we're not careful, we become too calloused or worn out to try.

We get worn out fighting with a strong-willed child.

We get worn out waiting for the apology we think we deserved and never got.

We get worn out struggling with a distant spouse.

We get worn out holding onto hurt until it festers and becomes an infection requiring intense treatment. Unaddressed disappointment is poison to the soul. When we ignore things out of fear, we grapple with the pain of crumbling emotions.

When our "want-to" is worn out, it's tempting to write something off as beyond repair because the cure for our pain requires surrender.

In John 5, Jesus encountered a crippled man, lying mere inches from the waters of the Pool of Bethesda, alongside many others who wanted the healing properties they believed the waters offered. This man lived as an invalid for *thirty-eight years*. Worn out from 38 years of missed opportunities, he had nothing left to offer Jesus but excuses. "People go in ahead of me...no one helps me in." Before Jesus offered the cure, He asked a question: *"Do you want to get well?"* Jesus did in one moment what the man couldn't do in a lifetime.

Jesus offers us the cure of patience when we're worn out from fighting, forgiveness when we're worn out from waiting, and grace when we're worn out from struggling. He invites us to receive the remedy for our numb, tired hearts. What do we do when our "want-to" is worn out?

## THE CURE FOR A WORN-OUT WANT-TO IS SURRENDER

Surrender starts by following the same principles Jesus offers the despondent man in John 5.

**Get up.** Resist the temptation to concede defeat to the sting of pain and allow God to heal you. Jesus invites us to get up out of a victim mentality and get into His perspective.

**Pick up your mat**. In those four words, Jesus told the broken man, *"You don't belong here. Look to Me as your Healer and become who I created you to be."* Leave behind the paralysis of faulty beliefs by receiving God's truth.

**Walk.** What action step is God is calling you to take? Forgive others. Ask for grace. Stop doubting. Lay down pride. Embrace a fresh start by trusting in God's Word for guidance and the Holy Spirit for empowerment.

Just as Jesus restored a broken man, He can revive a worn out want-to. Don't put it off another moment. Step into surrender and see what God will do.

**Astounded,**

*Angela*

# THE EXPERIMENT

*"Jesus gave them this answer: "Very truly I tell you, the Son can do nothing by himself; he can do only what he sees his Father doing, because whatever the Father does the Son also does."* JOHN 5:19

My family hadn't laughed that hard in a long time. It was one of those *"doubled-over-snorting-through-your-nose-can't-catch-your-breath"* sort of laughs. Ok, maybe I felt a tad guilty that our raucous joy came at my husband's expense, but after an overscheduled month, we all needed it.

It started when my son, Christian, shared his highlight reel from youth camp. He regaled us with the kind of tales one might expect from a week where 27 junior and senior high boys shared a cabin. During one of the worship times, Christian tried something we dubbed, *"the experiment."*

*"I wonder. If I worship the same way my dad does, will anyone notice?"* he mused to himself. For just a moment, he intentionally imitated my husband's mannerisms during worship. Trust me, it was at that point in the story that I nearly voiced my disapproval at

his antics during a church service. But he's a great kid, and my husband and I gave him a little latitude, perhaps out of sheer curiosity.

*"What do you mean, you imitated me?"* my husband asked incredulously. *"I don't do anything in worship."* My son proceeded to respond with an animated reenactment of a typical Sunday morning. He even included descriptions for what he called—ahem—"Dad's moves."

**The one-step:** one foot in front of the other, shuffle style.

**The point up:** both hands pointer fingers up.

**The bounce:** up on the tiptoes.

**The right-hand drumstick:** perhaps he's playing along?

**The praying hands rub:** rub hands together in prayer position.

My daughter jumped in the action and affirmed my son's every observation. *"Yes! Dad does that!"* I'm aware you might find this whole scene a tad disrespectful, or maybe even sacrilegious. Please understand; my husband was *beside* himself laughing. He never gave his *"worship style"* a second thought, and Christian's imitation sent us into stitches. Later, I chided myself for not reprimanding him. And I heard God's gentle voice whisper these words:

> *"Your son watches your husband worship. He has observed him so intently, he can imitate his mannerisms. He could be watching his father do a lot of things that you would never want him to imitate, coming home drunk or speaking harshly to you. Think about that, Angela. He has studied his dad in worship to the point that he can replicate his every move."*

Wow. And, you know what? Five students came up to my son at camp with the same sentence: *"You worship just like your dad."*

In John Chapter 5, Jesus was questioned by the religious leaders of the day for healing on the Sabbath. He answered their inquisition this way in Verse 19:

*"Very truly I tell you, the Son can do nothing by himself; he can do only what he sees his Father doing, because whatever the Father does the Son also does."*

Words to live by. I'm incredibly grateful my son watched his dad worshipping his heart out because he's in love with Jesus. We are far from perfect parents, but I pray the positive images leave the most lasting impact on our son's life. The world is watching closely those of us who follow Jesus. Do they see us imitating Christ? Have I studied my Heavenly Father's character so closely that I can mirror His mannerisms? Perhaps an old camp song says it best: *"And they'll know we are Christians by our love, by our love; they will know we are Christians by our love."*

We may not know when someone is watching us, but as they do, they search for one thing: *"Do they look like their 'Dad'?"*

Do we choose to love like Jesus?

Do we take a stand for justice?

Do we look for ways to elevate others?

Do we watch our words?

Do we spend time in prayer?

Let's make it our goal to study the Word of God and the character of God until we can imitate His every move. The highest compliment anyone could ever give me?

*"You're just like your 'Dad'."*

**Astounded,**

*Angela*

# ZERO TO HERO

*"We're all like sheep who've wandered off and gotten lost. We've all done our own thing, gone our own way."*      ISAIAH 53: 6

Ok, I'm willing to admit when I'm wrong. I posted a *not-so-nice* comment on social media about a local department store after my frustration over a phone call rife with customer service faux pas. Despite the debacle, only this store carried a specific item of clothing we needed. Hosting an out-of-town family for a holiday weekend, I waited until the last minute to make the purchase. Armed with thinning patience and a crummy attitude, I headed to the mall. I hadn't shopped at this particular retailer in years. In my rush to judgement, I ruminated, *"Is it any wonder they're going under?"* Basically, in my book, they were a big fat *zero*. My pride took a hit the moment I walked through the doors.

"*Huh...look at that fabulous pair of pants...*" I mumbled to myself. *"Oh, my goodness, these prices are fantastic."* An hour later, I not only left with the item they graciously held at the front counter for me, but with an armful of clothes at a steal. "*Hmmm.*

*At these prices, I should head to their home store and pick up a couple more things we need."*

That's when I met Mary. She warmly assisted me and offered to hold my purchases while I ran to one more store. *"Here, how about this?"* she suggested as she circled a number on my receipt. *"Just call this number and ask for me, Mary, when you're ready. Pull your car around to this entrance and I'll load up your purchases on a dolly and bring them to you!"* Yeah, that was the point I wanted to crawl in a hole. To say I was embarrassed by my rush to judgement is an understatement. But wait, it gets better.

I finished shopping and drove around to the outside entrance she described. However, I couldn't figure out where it was to save my life. Hot, late, and lost, I sheepishly called Mary. She stayed on the phone with me until I found it. She loaded my purchases—including some from another store—onto a dolly, rolled that thing through the mall, and even put my purchases in my trunk for me. While my behavior smacked of a *zero*, Mary turned out to be a hero.

I drove away with my head hanging, pride wounded, and lesson learned. I deleted my original post, but the damage was done. I shared my experience with our guests over baked beans and corn casserole, but all I really tasted was shame. Mary painstakingly aided me when I was desperately lost. She didn't vent frustration, make me carry my own packages, or call it quits. Nope. She demonstrated the best customer service I witnessed in a long time. She also modeled something else: grace.

Over dinner, my brother-in-law shared how vital it is for those who call themselves Christians to compassionately share Jesus with those who are lost. *"Lost,"* I said to myself. Images of me frantically driving around a mall I've been to 300 times flashed through my mind. I wondered out loud: if someone doesn't have a personal relationship with Jesus Christ, they're lost and in need of a Savior, just like I was before I met Christ. The last thing someone needs when they're lost is a good old-fashioned scolding about *"how lost they are, and for goodness sake can't they get 'un-lost'?"*

**They need someone like Mary: someone who will stay on the phone, carry their baggage, and meet them where they are.**

When was the last time I showed that kind of compassion to someone who was lost? It's so much easier to rush to judgement and label someone a zero than to show grace. Yet, that's exactly what Jesus does for us. What if we saw people and a broken world through God's eyes? What if we chose grace? The words of Isaiah 53 encourage us to love like our hero, Jesus.

> *"We're all like sheep who've wandered off and gotten lost. We've all done our own thing, gone our own way. And God has piled all our sins, everything we've ever done wrong, on Him. Still, it's what God had in mind all along, to crush Him with pain. The plan was that He give Himself as an offering for sin so that He'd see life come from it—life, life and more life."*

**Astounded,**

*Angela*

# WHEN A PROMISE IS STUCK IN TRANSIT

*"Those that wait upon the Lord shall renew their strength; they shall mount up with wings as eagles; they shall run, and not be weary; they shall walk, and not faint."*  ISAIAH 40:31

I chuckled when I noticed them lying on my kitchen counter. The lost luggage tags shouted "RUSH" in bright red letters, but the garment bag had other plans. My husband boarded a plane for a quick 2-day turnaround to speak at a church in Canada. Who knew, however, that Newark, New Jersey would prove so much more interesting to his suitcase than Toronto? Alas, Dale preached an alternate message in a borrowed shirt since both his suit and illustration were in his luggage. A couple dozen phone calls and six days later, the wayward bag arrived safely back on our front porch.

The tags ended up in the trash, but not before they made me do more than smile. They made me think about the many times

I wished God would send an answer with "RUSH" delivery. Does it ever feel like your promise is stuck in transit? Why is waiting so hard? Sometimes I see myself in the actions of the bratty little girl in Willy Wonka. *"I want a golden goose and I want it now!"* she shouts impetuously. I can't say I've ever screamed for a golden goose, but I have found myself on the verge of a tantrum when I'm forced to wait.

**We can all relate to the wait.** We wait with bated breath for college acceptance letters. We wait with knots in our stomach for pathology reports. We wait with wilted hope for a prodigal child. And while we wait, our emotions run the gamut from *"mildly inconvenienced"* to *"hanging on by a thread."* Confusion, frustration, or anxiety can choke out our trust in God. It's wishful thinking to put 100% of your trust in an airline; but it's foolish to put anything less than 100% of your trust in God.

We can't see what God sees so we don't always understand His timetable. Our souls can grow tired waiting on a delayed promise. Isn't it encouraging to know that God is patient with us, even in our impatience? Isaiah 40:31 is healing balm for a heavy heart:

*"Those that wait upon the Lord shall renew their strength; they shall mount up with wings as eagles; they shall run, and not be weary; they shall walk, and not faint."*

Weary…faint…in need of strength…telltale signs of a depleted spirit. Let's face it, life can serve up far more agonizing experiences than lost luggage. Waiting requires us to relinquish control. The enemy tempts us to believe that the absence of visible activity means the lack of the presence of God. In God's schedule, waiting is never wasted. He longs to teach us to trust His character even when we don't see the fulfilment of a promise. Sometimes His answer is yes, sometimes His answer is no, and many times His answer is *not yet.* We're encouraged through many Biblical examples of men and women who waited faithfully and held on to the promises of God. Is waiting worth it?

## CONSIDER WHAT HAPPENS IN THE WAITING

**Our character is tested.** Abraham waited for a son and God made him the father to many nations. God develops our character and transforms it into His likeness.

**Our motives are refined.** Joseph waited for freedom and God elevated him from the prison to the palace. God examines our motives and purifies our hearts.

**Our fear is exposed.** David waited for God's timing and God made him King. God uproots worry and replaces it with peace.

**Our faith is deepened.** Daniel waited in the lion's den and God delivered him and blessed him. God demonstrates His power and promotes us into greater favor.

**Our priorities are realigned.** Paul waited years to begin his ministry after encountering Jesus on the Road to Damascus. God used him to write two-thirds of the New Testament and bring the Gospel to the world. God changes us from the inside out and uses us for His glory.

**Our destiny is defined.** We, the Bride of Christ, wait with anticipation for His return. This is not all there is. God's ultimate destiny is eternity in heaven with Him. And that, my friend, is worth waiting for.

Don't despair when it seems a promise is stuck in transit. Place your hope fully in God to prove Himself faithful while you wait. His promises may not come with "RUSH" tags, but His timing is always, always perfect.

**Astounded,**
*Angela*

# A HALLMARK CHRISTMAS MOVIE GONE ROGUE

*"While they were there, the time came for the baby to be born, and she gave birth to her firstborn, a son. She wrapped him in cloths and placed him in a manger, because there was no guest room available for them."*                                    LUKE 2:6-7

I love a good Hallmark Christmas movie. These sappy stories lure hopeless romantics with the promise of nostalgia and a happy ending. I'm clearly aware that the plot is set to "repeat," with a girl—usually from a big city—meeting some small-town boy in a place called something akin to Wonderland Lodge. Sparks fly, only to be interrupted by the boyfriend who wants none of the Christmas spirit. Alas! Our heroine discovers she *does* want to live in a one-stoplight town after all! In this idyllic setting, Christmas isn't complete without hot chocolate and ice skating. And each movie ends the same way: our star-crossed couple kiss in the moonlight. Or in a horse-drawn sleigh. Or in the snow-laden cottage. You get the picture.

These predictable movies deliver on one thing: warm, fuzzy feelings dunked in eggnog and wrapped with a shiny, red bow. Yet real life is anything but predictable. And one year, our Christmas was a Hallmark movie gone rogue.

Festive wreaths decked every door and handcrafted poinsettia napkin holders donned my dinner table. Snow globes...nativity sets...stockings and reindeer. And the pièce de résistance? The Christmas tree. Not just any tree—*a freshly cut blue spruce*, lovingly chosen at our favorite tree lot as our breath filled the crisp, December air. We decorated her branches while carols rang in the background. Our kids snapped photos of the ornaments made by tinier hands in years gone by. I climbed into bed relishing the scenes that fit nicely into my Hallmark film.

I woke to swollen eyes, a runny nose, and a burning throat. *"UGHHHHHH,"* I thought to myself. *"I'm allergic to the tree. Give it a day. I'm sure my symptoms will subside."* Three days later, I realized the inevitable: either the tree had to move, or I did. I studied every ornament and started the unthinkable: I took every single one off and laid them on the stairs.

I begged my husband to find a new home for our precious tree on the deck outside. *"At least I can see the Christmas lights through the kitchen window,"* I whimpered. I proceeded to carry the white, fake tree (fully decorated I might add), up from the basement. The tree separated into sections, ornaments crashing to the floor and the base breaking in two. I plopped down on the steps to pick up broken pieces of a glass snowflake. *"Where's the ice-skating rink? The horse-drawn sleigh? The homemade mittens?"*

Nowhere. Just a harried mom trying to gather the remnants of a fallen-apart fake tree because she's the poster child for Allegra. At this point, I may or may not have shed a few tears. The next morning, I admired our 25-year old collection of ornaments outside, under the gazebo on the deck. I glanced into the living room and smiled at the replacement impostor, held together by super glue and ingenuity.

And that, folks, is real life. Sometimes families fight and turkeys burn, and moms are allergic to their one-of-a-kind, evergreen Christmas tree. Sometimes the best of intentions go rogue and we unwrap disappointment alongside Legos and socks. Sometimes the only predictable plot is the one that includes the unpredictable.

On my trips to Israel, I visited a little town called Bethlehem. In this humble place, a King would be born—not in a palace or filmed by Hollywood—but in an obscure cave witnessed by lowly shepherds. A young girl named Mary and her husband, Joseph, welcomed the Savior of the world surrounded by sheep and feeding troughs. Unexpected. Uninvited. Undone. Yet exactly what God intended.

## SOMETIMES OUR UNDONE MOMENTS ARE GOD'S INTENDED MIRACLES

Sometimes life goes rogue. Sometimes the kids don't want to come home for the holidays and hearts shatter like glass snowflakes. Sometimes, death steals a loved one and Christmas seems hollow. Yet, somehow, God births a miracle. He gives strength to weather adversity, and grace to bear heartache.

Because Christ came into our unpredictable mess, we have hope. I pray His love breathes new life into tender places. And I pray, dear friend, that you are not allergic to your Christmas tree.

**Astounded,**

*Angela*

# MY BORROWED LIFE—MOMENTS FROM KENYA

*"Love is patient."*                    1 CORINTHIANS 13:4

I have another life. It's a life I love but it's not a life I own. It's a borrowed life; on loan from the African soil. It isn't mine to keep.

It's a life where a rooster unapologetically announces the morning and simple moments tug at my arm to take notice. Home cooked breakfasts invite me to linger and uneven steps warn me to walk cautiously. My pace slows. My eyes adjust to absorb markets strewn with yellow bananas, hanging meat and local wares. Clothing lines dressed in vivid colors don the landscape while preparations for someone's dinner fill the thick air with smoke.

The drone of convenience and comfort that normally dulls my senses is replaced by jarring doses of inconvenience and uncertainty. They demand I draw from dormant reserves of ingenuity and patience.

## PATIENCE—A SLOWED, DIFFERENT LIFE

Patience when water doesn't flow, turning a shower into an event. Patience when each meal is painstakingly selected from market to table and cooked from scratch. Freshly cut mango, stewed okra, seasoned rice, boiled cabbage...patience when tilapia is served whole and succulent pieces of fish must be carefully separated from bone. Patience to sip homemade masala tea, rich with warm milk and spices. Patience when Wi-Fi is scarce and conversations across a dinner table eclipse the addiction to the Internet.

Patience when riding in a car driven by someone who is—thankfully—exceptionally adept at crossing dirt roads deeply rutted by the African rains. Someone with a story; a story that steals my heart like a thief. Someone like Livingston, who faithfully provides transportation to serve his church, and in turn, me. Patience while he waits in faith for God to heal his wife from infertility. Each morning my drive includes a smile, a kind word, and a gentle nudge to expand my Swahili.

**Every corner tells a new story: women whose bravery exceeds any courage I have ever known, and whose prayers reveal a depth of relationship with Jesus I honestly covet.**

Women like Jane, who fights a difficult battle with heart problems yet designs breathtaking jewelry for God's glory—all at the tender age of eighteen. Her maturity humbles me. Women like Terry, who survived a brutal rape on her wedding day only to tragically lose her husband a month after she eventually married. Her radiant spirit wrecks me.

I stand in their shadow. This is a borrowed life. I borrow their strength, their dignity, their resolve, their tenacity, their wisdom, their beauty. I marvel at the grace God has appointed to them and the anointing that has come at such a price.

## THESE PEOPLE—THIS PLACE

The unspoiled land of the Maasai Mara whose glorious sounds and austere silence simultaneously leave me awestruck. Where crickets sound like wind chimes and the horizon stretches farther than the eye can see. Truly, we all only borrow this place. *A slowed, different life.*

Patience in the tan grass to see if the stealth cheetah will attempt a run at the gazelle. Patience on the Mara Riverbank while thousands of wildebeests and zebras choose their moment to cross during migration. Patience won after eleven hours of driving and waiting on these indecisive, complicated animals. We witnessed the truly magnificent. At the end of our unforgettable day, Robert, our game drive guide, summed up the lesson God taught me from this trip to Africa in four words. *"Timing and patience matter."*

Africa. These moments that press themselves so intensely into my heart I feel as if I cannot breathe. This undoing that has forever marked me. This captivating call that has ruined me for a life with any hint of complacency. This borrowed life that pulls me toward patience, mostly with myself. Africa has wound her fingers so tightly around my skin, I can only wear her home. I can only hope I step into these shoes I have borrowed and walk worthy of all God has allowed me to see. To hear. To know.

Africa has been my teacher, my friend, my most unlikely companion. She reminds me to live this one life I am given with reckless abandon and ridiculous gratitude. She loves me without hesitation and teaches me to love without reservation.

*This is a life we can all borrow: one that lives wisely and loves well.*

**Astounded,**

*Angela*

# CHURCH?
# WHY BOTHER?

*"The body is a unit, though it is made up of many parts; and though all its parts are many, they form one body. So it is with Christ."* 1 CORINTHIANS 12:12

My heart sank when I read it. Recent statistics tell us less than 25% of Americans attend church. Many never set foot inside a church. Some were hurt and left. Still others would go if someone would only invite them. My husband and I devoted our lives to ministry, and have pastored River of Life Church in Virginia for over two decades. Although online church affords an alternative platform for spiritual growth, it isn't a substitute for community. I was more than a bit bothered by American's "Church? Why Bother?" attitude. People share a myriad of reasons they avoid church.

*They're all hypocrites anyway.*

*I'm way too busy on the weekends and Sunday is my down day.*

*I came a couple times and didn't get anything out of it. Plus, I don't think anyone has missed me.*

I've heard all of these explanations, and more, firsthand. You won't find a perfect church because no person is perfect. One of the reasons God created the church is community. We grow as we serve each other, use our gifts, and reach the lost. Why bother? My injured knee might make the point best. Years ago, I tore my meniscus. You couldn't see it without a MRI, but on a hike through the Shenandoah Mountains, the downhill trek became painful. That small tear screamed at me with every step. It required cortisone injections and surgery to repair the damage. That one tiny tear affected my whole body. It altered my attitude, hampered my ability to exercise normally, and disturbed my sleep. Who would've thought that such a small body part would have such a big part to play?

God designed the *body* of Christ to function best when all of us do our part. No one is small. No role is insignificant. A church needs unity, and diversity, to function properly. When you're not part of a church, the body of Christ suffers. With all her imperfections, the Church is the Body of Christ. Look at the picture Paul painted in 1 Corinthians 12:12, 14-27.

> *"The body is a unit, though it is made up of many parts; and though all its parts are many, they form one body. So it is with Christ. Now the body is not made up of one part but many. If the foot should say, 'Because I am not a hand, I do not belong to the body,' it would not for that reason cease to be part of the body. And if the ear should say, 'Because I am not an eye, I do not belong to the body,' it would not for that reason cease to be part of the body. If the whole body were an eye, where would the sense of hearing*

*be? If the whole body were an ear, where would the sense of smell be? But in fact God has arranged the parts in the body, every one of them, just as He wanted them to be. There should be no division in the body, but that its parts should have equal concern for each other. If one part suffers, every part suffers with it; if one part is honored, every part rejoices with it. Now you are the body of Christ, and each one of you is a part of it."*

This passage tells us why we should bother. You are valuable. Your gifts and presence are needed in the Body of Christ. Sure, we can come up with a list of excuses to avoid church. But Christ died for the church and He loves the church. Aren't we grateful that His response to our need for a Savior wasn't, *"Why Bother?"*

The church is us: you and me. If you're not plugged into a church, I pray this encouraged you to look for one this week. If you're already committed to a local church community, invite someone to come with you. If online is the only option for you in this season, connect to a small group. *Why bother? Because Christ bothered for me.*

**Astounded,**

*Angela*

# DODGE DISTRACTION

*"She had a sister called Mary, who sat at the Lord's feet listening to what he said. But Martha was distracted by all the preparations that had to be made."*
LUKE 10:39-40

It was not my finest hour. I got ready in a rush, downed a cup of coffee, and dashed to the church for a leadership conference we hosted. My mind raced...

*Does my daughter have money for her appointment?*

*Did I let the dog out?*

*Do we have the handouts our speaker wants?*

*Does this new outfit look okay?*

I parked my car behind the church, grabbed my purse, and hurried in to help make last minute preparations. One small problem: I left my car running. *For seven hours.* When my husband left the building that afternoon to take our speaker back to the hotel, he heard the purr of my car engine. As he leaned down to confirm his suspicions, he nearly scalded his face on the overheated hood. After the vehicle cooled down, I drove it safely home. I'm grateful it wasn't worse. I had just put gas in my car the night before, so it didn't run out. And despite 90-degree temperatures, the engine didn't burn up. Yet, I left completely bewildered as to how I could have possibly done such a thing. Honestly, I didn't even remember getting out of my car. I was rushed. Racing. And dangerously distracted.

I learned a powerful lesson that day: **Don't underestimate distraction.**

Distraction is one of our greatest adversaries. A distracted driver can take a wrong turn, swerve lanes, or get in a wreck. A distracted life can strain relationships, weaken our purpose, and pillage our faith. I love the tale of two sisters in Luke 10:38-42.

> *"As Jesus and his disciples were on their way, he came to a village where a woman named Martha opened her home to him. She had a sister called Mary, who sat at the Lord's feet listening to what he said. But Martha was distracted by all the preparations that had to be made. She came to him and asked, 'Lord, don't you care that my sister has left me to do the work by myself? Tell her to help me!' 'Martha, Martha,' the Lord answered, 'you are worried and upset about many things, but few things are needed—or indeed only one. Mary has chosen what is better, and it will not be taken away from her."*

Martha was distracted. And honestly, if I hosted Jesus and the disciples for dinner, I'd probably be preoccupied and stressed out, too. Yet, what Jesus really wanted from Martha was one thing Mary offered: her presence. Distraction is defined as *"that which divides the attention or prevents concentration."* If we don't learn to dodge distraction, not only do we risk mental, physical and emotional fatigue; we miss meaningful moments. It takes determination to dodge distraction. Since distraction shrouds itself in so many forms, identify what tends to distract you and develop strategies to avoid it.

## IMPLEMENT THESE THREE TIPS
## TO ELUDE THE DANGER OF DISTRACTION

**Start your day with God.** Offer Jesus the one thing He really wants: your presence. Discipline yourself to spend time in prayer and God's Word before you turn on the computer, dive into work, or get on your phone. Ask God to help you focus on His plans for your day.

**Slow down.** Practice deep breathing, which decelerates your heart rate, lowers your blood pressure, and improves mental clarity. Instead of staring down an overscheduled day, adjust your pace and leave margin so you can hear God's voice.

**Set limits.** Establish boundaries, asking for accountability in areas that cause you the most temptation. If social media or scrolling the internet tends to divert you for hours, set a timer. Allocate an area in your home for work projects to maintain balance and give relationships top priority.

That embarrassing experience taught me the value of giving your undivided attention. Let's focus on Jesus this week and dodge the danger of distraction. One more thing: take your keys out of the ignition before you leave your car.

**Astounded,**

*Angela*

# MAKE ROOM
# FOR OTHERS

*"Therefore, as God's chosen people, holy and dearly loved, clothe yourselves with compassion, kindness, humility, gentleness and patience."* COLOSSIANS 3:12

Insecurity is ugly. When I've found myself on the receiving end of someone's insecurity-laced actions, it stung. When, through my words or behavior, I made someone else feel small, I hung my head in shame. When we feel insecure about ourselves, we compensate with tactics that belittle or bully those we see as a threat. Insecurity fixates on style over substance. We wrestle with discontent with our lot in life when we covet the blessings of others. We wince at our friends' social media feeds when our life seems so dull.

The dirty little secret? We all have areas of insecurity; places where fear preys on our weaknesses and plagues our strengths.

What if we focused more on celebrating each other and less on competing? We don't have to allow insecurity to coil itself around our heart. Instead, we can clothe ourselves with the character of God. If you want to experience God's favor, sow favor into the lives of others.

**Maybe you're the smartest person in the room.** They won't remember how much you know, they'll remember how you made them feel.

**Maybe you're the prettiest person in the room.** Pretty is as pretty does and kindness is your must-have accessory.

**Maybe you're the most physically fit person in the room.** Don't worry so much about running circles around them and look for ways to go the extra mile.

**Maybe you're the most talented person in the room.** Use your gifts to elevate others.

Insecurity doesn't have to win. Immerse yourself in the Word and you'll know your worth in Christ. Colossians 3:12 shares five character traits that help ground our identity in Christ and guard us from wounding others.

*"Therefore, as God's chosen people, holy and dearly loved, clothe yourselves with compassion, kindness, humility, gentleness and patience."*

Compassion reflects a genuine concern and sympathy for the pain of others. Kindness is both considerate and generous without asking for anything in return. Gentleness shows a mild and tender temperament, bringing peace into overheated spaces. Patience tolerates delays without becoming annoyed or anxious. Humility is defined as, *"a modest or low view of one's own importance."*

We combat insecurity by emulating the character of Christ. He is our greatest example of humility, leaving heaven to take the form of a servant. He modeled what it looks like to elevate others.

People *felt* important to Him because they *were* important to Him. He dialogued with a religious leader, Nicodemus, in private, to answer his questions and lead him to salvation. He called a despised tax collector, Zacchaeus, out of a tree, and joined him in his home for dinner and life-changing conversation. He cooked breakfast for a wayward disciple, Peter, and restored him through grace. He sat in the dirt at a well in Samaria to have the longest recorded conversation in Scripture with a broken, marginalized woman. She became the first female evangelist in history. These stories simply scratch the surface of the way Jesus showed us how to live.

**Jesus was *always* the most important person in the room; but He made room for others.** He lifted others—out of darkness, out of complacency, and out of bondage to sin. On the night He was betrayed, He knelt to wash the disciples' feet; even those of Judas. On the cross, He prayed that His Father would forgive those who crucified Him. On resurrection day, He broke the power of the grave to give us the promise of eternal life. When we know who we are in Christ, we become Christ to others.

Don't be enticed by insecurity. When you choose to follow Christ, God's hand is on your life. Clothe yourself with humility; look for opportunities to elevate others. What you make happen for others, God will make happen for you. He makes a way when there doesn't seem to be a way. Let your presence shift the atmosphere in a room as you make room for others.

**Astounded,**

*Angela*

# RELEASE THE POWER OF PRAISE

*"About midnight Paul and Silas were praying and singing hymns to God, and the other prisoners were listening to them. Suddenly there was such a violent earthquake that the foundations of the prison were shaken. At once all the prison doors flew open, and everyone's chains came loose."* ACTS 16:25-26

In 2003, I began to feel ill and experience sharp pain I had never known before. I had no appetite and struggled for several months, losing weight and enduring bouts of excruciating abdominal pain. After many doctor visits, I was admitted to the hospital. My heart rate had plummeted to 41 beats per minute and my blood pressure was hovering dangerously low at 76/40. I spent 11 days in the hospital with nothing to eat or drink and was scheduled for an extensive MRI. I lay on my side in a fetal position, completely alone, and watched the screen as the barium reached my stomach and stopped. The 45-minute test took seven hours.

As I lay on the cold, metal table, hour after hour, I felt like a wrung-out rag doll. I heard the Lord say to me, *"Angela, I know you can worship Me on the platform. I want to know if you can worship me here."* The hospital room became holy ground. I sang quietly with tears flowing down my face, *"Here I am to worship, Here I am to bow down, Here I am to say that You're my God."* That moment of surrender ushered in my miracle.

A team of specialists made the diagnosis of Superior Mesenteric Artery Syndrome.

SMA Syndrome is a rare, life-threatening disorder where the superior mesentery takes too sharp of a right turn. The first portion of my intestines was compressing the artery and acting as an obstruction. Doctors performed serious, complicated surgery to bypass the affected portion of my intestines and relieve pressure on the artery. Then, they reconnected my stomach to a lower section of the intestines. Recovery included long months unable to eat solid food, healing from trauma, and adjusting to a scar that runs the length of my torso. God taught me through that dark season to trust His character and worship Him no matter what. Through health challenges and times of adversity, I learned to release the power of praise.

In Acts 16, while Paul and Silas were in the city of Philippi, they were delivered from prison through the power of praise. On their way to find a place to pray, Paul freed a slave girl from a demon which had allowed her to make prophecies about the future. This angered those who profited from her ability which was lost once the demon was gone.

**The people's response was prison.** They brought charges that Paul and Silas were breaking Roman laws on religion. Paul and Silas are seized, dragged, stripped, severely flogged and thrown into the inner cell of a prison. Hands and feet in stocks, backs bleeding, they had every reason to be angry and ask God to get them out of this unfair situation. But they did none of that.

**Paul and Silas' response was praise.** At midnight, during their darkest moment, they are up *"praying and singing hymns to God."* In the middle of unimaginable pain, they expressed gratitude. Remember that Paul and Silas were looking for a place of prayer, and they found it right here, even in a prison. Their praise became a weapon.

**When our response is praise, God's response is power.** God sent such a violent earthquake that the prison doors flew open. This is the power of praise: chains break...doors open. The jailer reached for his sword to kill himself, fearing the prisoners would all escape. Paul and Silas yelled for him to stop and didn't leave even when they had the chance. Why? Because they were others-minded and Kingdom-minded.

**The jailer's response was petition.** A prison became a place of freedom. Incredulous, the jailer asked, *"What must I do to be saved?"* Paul and Silas' witness and integrity preached a silent sermon that led to the salvation of the jailor and his entire family. In the morning, Paul and Silas were released.

Praise isn't chained by a prison. Or a hospital room. Or a fractured relationship. Or a financial crisis. We can encounter the presence of God anytime we choose to respond to trials with praise. Praise invites God's blessing and releases God's power. When we praise, God acts. God turns our midnight moments into miracles.

**Astounded,**
*Angela*

# COURAGE FOR SLIDING ROCK TRAIL

*"And who is the Rock besides our God? It is God who arms me with strength and keeps my way secure. You make Your saving help my shield; Your help has made me great. You provide a broad path for my feet so my ankles do not give way."*    PSALM 18:31-36

Ten days. Five states. Two family reunions. Welcome to another Donadio vacation, filled with enough adrenaline-pumping experiences to satisfy this adventure junkie. I braved frigid water temperatures to ride the waves in Virginia Beach. I traded my wave board for paddles to white water raft down the Nantahala River in Tennessee. And once we settled in Georgia for a few days, Tallulah Gorge called my name.

She lures countless tourists through her breathtaking beauty and challenging terrain, including some in our extended family who hiked several miles around and down into the gorge. We stopped to marvel at breathtaking waterfalls, crossed a suspension bridge, and descended half of the 1099 metal stairs required to reach the gorge floor. However, when we arrived at the small, wooden gate providing brave souls the option to explore remote sections of the gorge, we found it locked due to severe early morning thunderstorms. For some of us, the chance to experience something only a few get to see proved impossible to resist.

Two days later, a handful of us returned to score some of the 100 allotted daily permits. We hiked back down the stairs, traversed the bridge, and used our golden ticket to get through the gate. We continued the dangerous trek 1000-feet deep into the gorge floor and climbed through the boulder-filled Sliding Rock Trail to the Bridal Falls Waterfall. About an hour in, my husband blurted out, *"This payoff better be something else."* In case you're wondering, the *"very strenuous"* description provided on the brochure was spot on. Ahem.

What on earth could be worth all that? Once you've arrived, you can use that coveted ticket to slide down the boulders and swim in Bridal Falls. *Spectacular.* Yep, the payoff was worth it. Tallulah Gorge may not be one of your bucket-list items, but we still have one thing in common: we won't get through life without courage.

## THE DEMANDING AND REWARDING EXPERIENCE REMINDED ME OF THREE CHOICES WE CAN ALL MAKE WHEN LIFE DEMANDS COURAGE

**Seize the opportunity.** Too often, we stop at the locked, wooden gates of life because the sacrifice is too high, and the cost is too great. But when we do, we run the risk of missing a God-moment. Ask God for the courage to share your story with someone who needs Christ. Take every opportunity to make a difference in the lives of others.

**Stay low to the ground.** The best advice we received during our training orientation was to *"stay low to the ground."* Most injuries come when people try to stand up and walk when the slippery, rough terrain requires a low center of gravity. It's better to come out with a sore backside and bruised palms than a concussion or broken bones. Center yourself by staying low to the ground through consistent prayer and worship.

**Don't quit.** Our instructor called the last leg, *"the longest quarter mile you'll ever hike."* He wasn't lying. Unable to see the top as we scaled the 45-degree angled stone wall, we wondered if it would ever end. Perhaps you're trekking through the arduous last quarter mile—not of a trail, but of a trial. Don't quit; victory is just ahead.

Sometimes, life feels an awful lot like Sliding Rock Trail. Relationships get rocky. Financial challenges get slippery. Health problems plague our path. Perhaps you're facing a situation that's asking more of you than you think is humanly possible. Psalm 18:31-36 encourages us to find our brave in Jesus:

> *"And who is the Rock besides our God? It is God who arms me with strength and keeps my way secure. You make Your saving help my shield; Your help has made me great. You provide a broad path for my feet so my ankles do not give way."*

Even more than I'm an adrenaline junkie, I'm a Jesus junkie. I can't get enough of Him. Let His guiding presence and reassuring voice enable you to seize opportunities, stay low to the ground, and find your courage in Him.

**Astounded,**

*Angela*

# SEE THE UNSEEN

*"So do not fear, for I am with you; do not be dismayed, for I am your God. I will strengthen you and help you; I will uphold you with my righteous right hand."*     ISAIAH 41:10

*"Can we have your insurance card to update our information?"* the receptionist inquired.

*"Hmmm...I don't think anything has changed,"* I mumbled.

*"Well...it has been four years since you've been here, so maybe we should look at it just in case?"*

*"Four years?"* I thought to myself incredulously. *"FOUR YEARS? Epic fail on seeing the retinal specialist once a year, Angela."*

I could give you a dozen reasons as to why I put off seeing this particular doctor. No slight to him, but I'm not a fan of the disorienting routine of numbing drops, eye pressure gauges, new-fangled machines that flash jarring, blue specs, and examinations with blinding white light. Then there's the joyous experience of dilating my eyes, fumbling through the office space without my contacts, and listening to him dictate a stream of gibberish to his nurse while my heartbeat throbs in my ears.

More than a decade ago, I noticed a black spot in my left eye while on a family vacation. Within a few hours, I realized that something was terribly wrong with my vision. My first encounter with this retinal specialist revealed the price of being severely near-sighted. Over time, my retina stretched painfully thin, allowing microscopic blood vessels to hemorrhage, causing dark spots and blurred vision. The specialist performed a sophisticated procedure, using intravenous dye to find the source of the hemorrhage and lasers to repair it. Unfortunately, damage from scar tissue rendered my left eye useless except for peripheral vision. As a result, I'm supposed to see him every year, for signs of further damage in my left eye—or even worse—signs of damage in my right.

If I'm honest, in spite of all the explanations I could offer as to why four years have passed since my last visit, the core reason is fear. Dread hovers over me in the days leading up to my appointment. I'm afraid of what he's going to say. I'm afraid of what he's *not* going to say. Since there's nothing I can do to prevent the same thing from happening to my right eye, the thought of becoming blind is legitimate—and terrifying. Simply navigating the hours following dilation makes me feel frail and helpless. Not able to read music, or see my children walk down the aisle? Heartbreaking.

As I reflected on my appointment, God nudged me to deal with my fear. Learning to step scared in the face of genuine terror is no small feat. Courage is not the absence of fear, but the ability to move forward in spite of it. The narrative of so many powerful men and women in the Bible comforts us with the same four words that consoled their anxious hearts: *"Do not be afraid."*

Yet, God's words don't end with a directive; they end with a promise: *"For I am with you."* Fear renders us severely near-sighted and clouds our vision. It blinds us to the truth of a loving Heavenly Father who is wholly trustworthy when life is not. When the challenges of life disorient us and try to steal our peace, we can place our hope firmly in God.

## FEAR CLOUDS OUR VISION, BUT FAITH SEES THE UNSEEN

Whatever your future may hold, know that it cannot obscure your ability to see the sustaining grace of our Heavenly Father. You can choose faith. You can walk fearlessly knowing that your future is securely in His hands. Jesus died so we don't have to be held captive to fear. No darkness...no sickness...no confusion...no trial...no disappointment...is greater than His love for us. Don't let fear cloud your vision. Ask God for the faith to see the unseen, the courage to step scared, and the grace to trust Him no matter what.

**Astounded,**

*Angela*

# REBOUND FROM REJECTION

*"Am I now trying to win the approval of human beings, or of God? Or am I trying to please people? If I were still trying to please people, I would not be a servant of Christ."*     GALATIANS 1:10

I tried to ignore the lump forming in my throat and willed the corners of my mouth upwards into an awkward smile. My eyes darted across the top of the bleachers in a desperate attempt to avoid looking directly at her face. The thump of my heartbeat nearly drowned out her booming voice.

And, just as she had in every other middle school P.E. class, my teacher finally called my name: last. Whether the day's activity involved dodgeball or chin-ups, my 5'5" 12-year-old, slightly overweight, awkward frame struggled at all things requiring tennis shoes and a gymnasium floor. I got used to hearing my name picked last for a team, but I never quite got comfortable with the sting of rejection.

My dread of anything athletic became so intense that I literally let the pitcher hit me with a ball in a high school P.E. game to avoid the painful prospect of running the bases. True story. It wasn't until my college years that I turned a corner. While training for the Miss America program, I voluntarily took a college course that required running. Around a track. In tennis shoes. The first day, I trotted my out-of-shape body around one lap, holding my side and gasping for breath. But in a matter of three months, determination beat rejection: I ran an 8-minute mile and scored an A.

Years later, in 2011, I wished that my middle school P.E. teacher watched me climb Mt. Kilimanjaro to put in clean water wells. I was sure that rejection was now firmly a thing of the past. But rejection shows up uninvited in more places than a polished gym floor. It shows up on Saturday nights when you're scrolling social media and realize you weren't included in friends' plans. It shows up at offices when your boss overlooks your hard work on a project and chooses someone else. It shows up in living rooms when your husband confides he's having an affair and wants a divorce.

Wherever rejection rears its ugly head, it can take a bite out of our identity and cause us to question our worth. Fear of rejection wraps its tentacles around our hearts, imploring us to guard against future damage. As an author, the process of sending my first manuscript to publishers became fertile ground for rejection. God doesn't intend for us to go through life wrecked by rejection. Instead, we can rebound by discovering valuable insights.

**Rejection can wreck us or redirect us; the choice is ours.**

## HOW CAN WE REBOUND FROM REJECTION?

**Recognize fallout.** Rejection can cause us to question what we did wrong or wonder what's wrong with us. It is dangerous to believe the lie that we are "less than" or unvalued. If the venom of rejection sets in, it can limit our ability to experience healthy relationships. As we become aware of our emotional reactions, we can give God time to heal and teach us ways to wean ourselves off the need for approval.

**Rely on faith.** Often, God uses rejection to redirect us when something or someone isn't His will or His timing. As we hold tight to God's promises, we remember that humans are flawed; God is flawless. Rejection teaches us how to be a friend to the friendless and develop a greater understanding of ways that we reject God.

**Rally through forward thinking.** Keep a growth mindset and refuse to give up. Sometimes that might mean going back to the drawing board by honing our strategy or developing our skill. When things don't turn out the way we thought they would, it's an opportunity for us to self-reflect and self-correct.

Take comfort knowing Jesus also suffered rejection by man. Rejection doesn't define you or take away an ounce of God's love for us. We find our identity in Him. You can rebound from rejection by trusting fully in God's unfailing love. Jesus will never, ever reject you.

**Astounded,**
*Angela*

# DELIVER KINDNESS CURBSIDE

*"Whoever pursues righteousness and kindness will find life, righteousness, and honor."*                    PROVERBS 21:21

*"What year is your Cadillac?"*, he asked curiously.

*"Umm, I'm not really sure. Would you believe it was a gift!"* I said politely, albeit preoccupied while attempting to place my sandwich order in the line at Subway.

Undeterred, he continued, *"Well, you know next year they're coming out with flashers."*

Silence.

*"You know, flashers, like the ones you don't have on right now."*

His words hung in the air somewhere between, *"sure, I'd like that toasted,"* and, *"add extra mayo."* In that split second, I realized he wasn't interested in my car. He was annoyed.

*"These three senior citizens had to walk around your car parked there on the curb and step up because you're blocking the entrance."*

The three senior citizens he was referring to were himself and two ladies, looking graciously uncomfortable.

I frequent the Subway, just a half-mile down from the church where I work, countless times, not once parking by the door. But that day, I dashed in to grab a sandwich so I could get back and finish a project. Phone in one hand and wallet in the other, I was a woman on a mission and, well, the curb just seemed a whole lot quicker than a parking space.

I felt my face flush and my mind race to a myriad of responses ranging from slightly dismissive to *annoyed right back at ya, guy.*

**And then, I thought of my parents.** They drove halfway across the country to spend six days to take in the sights and sounds of Washington D.C., and cram in a flurry of family festivities. They poured their time and talents into a night of music to bless our church. They traversed steps and stores. And when, on a whim, I got us tickets to the Washington Nationals Game, my dad walked around *the entire stadium* to park the car.

Somehow, all of that squeezed into that split second following his mild but intentional public scolding. And, instead of opting for curt, I was kind. And let me tell you something. Reaching for kindness was the best moment of my day.

I'm chagrined to admit that far too many times, my drive and deadlines steamroll right over kindness. Reaching for kindness takes a whole lotta strength and self-control. It also takes something that is painfully disappearing from our culture: honor. Honor is defined as a tangible symbol signifying approval or distinction. Honor acts.

*"Oh, my goodness,"* I responded, gently putting my hand on one of the woman's shoulders. *"I'm so sorry! I was rushing from*

*work and just didn't even think of how inconsiderate that was. My parents are in their seventies and I sure wouldn't want someone to do that to them."*

"Oh, it's okay," he said, his face softening. *"Just don't do it again,"* he reprimanded, with a twinkle in his eye.

Ouch. But I resolved to let honor win. Kindness was going to win.

*"I sure won't,"* I smiled back.

I moved to the cashier and spoke in hushed tones. *"Have they finished their order?"*

*"No,"* she whispered back.

*"Please add their order to mine."*

On the way out, I patted the man on the back and said quietly, *"Lunch is on me today. It's the least I can do. And I hope it's what someone would do for my parents."*

For a moment I think he was mortified, and then a wave of appreciation washed over his face. He pulled me aside and gave me a hug. *"Oh, thank you, you sure didn't need to do that. But please know that these three travelers from West Virginia sure are thankful."*

We create a culture of honor when we refuse to argue and resolve to elevate. We don't have to agree with someone to honor them. Reach for kindness; one small decision at a time. Oh, and don't park on the curb.

**Astounded,**
*Angela*

# IN A NEW YORK STATE OF MIND

*"In their hearts humans plan their course, but the Lord establishes their steps."* PROVERBS 16:9

New York City can swallow you whole if you're not careful. It can also teach some powerful life lessons if you're a willing student. When my daughter was in high school, I accompanied her to the Big Apple for a week of musical theatre training. Not surprisingly, the trip was filled with ample adventure and food for thought. As I settled back into my normal routine at home, something felt different. I woke up in my own bed and drove my car down local streets. I went to the gym where the front desk knows my name and took a deep breath outside without the sting of exhaust. It felt familiar. Safe. Comfortable.

Sounds great, right? I'm grateful for my home, my family, and the community I love. But sometimes your soul needs the rush of the unfamiliar to challenge the rut of your routine. Routines give us stability and structure. Yet, they can also leave us susceptible to the perils of boredom. The doldrums of routine can dull our senses and smother our curiosity. The monotony of life can cause us to become indifferent to the needs of others. Boredom jeopardizes marriages, traps teenagers, stifles creativity, and zaps zeal.

Instead, let's awaken our souls to the world around us. Let's allow God to order our steps. You don't have to travel far to beat boredom at its own game: you just need a New York state of mind. My visit to the city that never sleeps showed me how small adjustments can energize a tired marriage, transform an angsty teenager, and recharge your creative batteries.

## UPGRADE YOUR ROUTINE
## WITH THESE FIVE CHALLENGES

**Make a date with inconvenience.** I took a bus to NYC for the first time in my life. Inconveniences like longer than expected wait times, cramped quarters, and a seat that faced backwards, quickly put a dent in my selfish nature. A trip out of our comfort zone might just be the ticket to tackle our me-centered mindsets. *Challenge: Intentionally fight selfishness by making a date with inconvenience.*

**New York City is expensive but kindness costs you nothing.** You'll find no shortage of two things here: ways to spend money, and people who need kindness. No matter where you live, you come in contact daily with people who desperately need a kind word, a hot meal, or a helping hand. *Challenge: Look for opportunities to show kindness to someone today: your stressed store clerk, your cranky boss, or your tired spouse.*

**Get moving.** I opted out of using the elliptical machine in our windowless fitness center to walk a mile and take my first-ever Soul Cycle class. It was an intense, exhilarating workout that pushed me to my limits. Improve your routine by getting off the couch and into the adventure of pursuing health. It's worth it! *Challenge: Get moving. Walk around the neighborhood. Sweat it out in a fitness class. Just move.*

**Welcome silence into your day.** New York City overloads all five senses in five minutes. The glare of the lights, the never-ending noise, the pungent mixture of aromas, the feel of the hot pavement under your feet...she heightens your awareness to everything nearby. Sometimes, it's good to force yourself to feel that alive. It also helps you to appreciate the return of silence. *Challenge: Welcome silence into moments of your day. Close your eyes and take some deep breaths. Get alone with God without the distraction of a phone, computer, or noise. Silence is salve for your soul.*

**Create memories.** We visited Rice to Riches, notorious for a wide variety of rice puddings. Our cab ride from the hotel cost more than the dessert. I know, ridiculous. We tasted six unique flavors over laughter and conversation. Anyone can get a Ho-Ho from a vending machine. But a cab ride for rice pudding? Priceless. *Challenge—Create a memory. Plan a fun night with your kids, pack a picnic dinner for a date with your spouse, or bring a co-worker their favorite dessert.*

Let's stay alert to ways God might want to rearrange our routines. Let Him shift your plans. He created us for so much more than simply going through the motions. Let's show up to a life of purpose.

**Astounded,**

*Angela*

# DREAMS OF OLYMPIC GLORY

*"So David triumphed over the Philistine with a sling and a stone;
without a sword in his hand he struck down the Philistine and
killed him."*
1 SAMUEL 17:50

Twizzles. Quads. 580's. These strange words appear every four years and they can only mean one thing: The Winter Olympics.

Any other time, you'd never find me watching parallel slalom skiing. But the Olympics? I'll stay up until I'm bleary eyed to witness greatness. These athletes defy gravity and cheat death as they skate on razor-sharp blades, slide headfirst in the skeleton at breakneck speeds, and twist themselves 20 feet into the air on a snowboard.

I paced nervously alongside my husband and son as I watched Shaun White achieve his 3rd Olympic Gold Medal in South Korea. When he put down a nearly flawless third run, I screamed like a maniac, *"He did it! He did it!"* A devastating fall and injury just mere months earlier threatened to cut his Olympic hopes short, landing him in the hospital via helicopter and requiring 62 stiches to his face. It's mind-boggling to grasp the amount of grit, determination, and bravery it must have taken for him to get back on a snowboard. And then to top it all off, he won a Gold Medal. One of my favorite Olympic moments. Ever.

The Olympics are replete with heart-stopping, history-making events. As I witness death-defying feats, I think for a split second, *"I could do that. I could race downhill on skis like her. I'll put in some practice runs and next Winter Olympics, I'll be boarding that plane with Team USA."*

What in the world would generate that fraction of sheer insanity? Because they make it look easy. It's ludicrous to think I'd ever step foot inside the Olympic Village. But I can't help wondering how often I attempt to tackle spiritual mountains with nothing more than a wing and a prayer.

In our haste to move on to an opportunity, it's tempting to skip the process of preparation. We do ourselves, others, and the kingdom of God a disservice when we forge ahead without the necessary preparation.

In 1 Samuel 17, we read a story about an Olympic-sized feat with Olympic-sized glory. From the outside looking in, one might be tempted to believe David effortlessly picked up a slingshot and a stone to kill the most daunting military giant Israel had seen to date. He made it look easy. Effortless. And we witness greatness and think...*"I could take him. Just give me a slingshot. I've got this."* But without preparation, that is as much a recipe for disaster as putting my size nine feet into ski boots and barreling down a mountain at 45 miles-an-hour.

Before David ever met Goliath, he prepared himself mentally, physically, and spiritually. He was physically strong, building his confidence over time by killing a lion and a bear to protect his sheep. He was mentally tough, able to withstand when overlooked for battle by his own father for older, seemingly more qualified brothers. And he was spiritually solid, his faith firmly grounded in a God he *knew* would deliver no matter what. When his preparation finally met opportunity, he rose to the occasion and God granted him success.

There just aren't enough personal trainers on the planet to prepare me to join Team USA. But we can prepare ourselves for the spiritual mountains God wants us to traverse through discipline and perseverance. Where do you sense God prompting you to make a change? Ask the Holy Spirit for the self-control you need to follow through on each commitment. Remember that life is a marathon, not a sprint. We stand firm and persevere when we know God is in control. **You are an overcomer because God oversees the outcome.**

What opportunity stands in front of you? Don't let intimidation from the Goliaths of life keep you from fixing your eyes on Jesus. You never know what come-from-behind, 11th-hour epic moment God is orchestrating. Press into His faithfulness and place your hope firmly in His character.

We may never carry the Olympic torch or stand on a medal stand. But we can commit to God's process of training in our lives, preparing for greatness. And here's the clincher: let God define what greatness looks like for you. Then when preparation meets opportunity, you'll be ready.

**Astounded,**
*Angela*

# DO AWAY WITH DO-OVER DAYS

*"His divine power has given us everything we need for life and godliness through our knowledge of Him who called us by His own glory and goodness."* 2 PETER 1:3-4

If life came with a remote control, I would've worn out the rewind button. Ever gulped down regret and woke up with a stomachache? Those moments when you think...

*If only I could get a "do-over." Push rewind. Take back my words.*

After a flip-flop filled week of family vacation one summer, our kids left halfway through to attend church camps. In their absence, the beach condo seemed eerily quiet, filled only with the gentle sound of ocean waves lapping the shore. Oh, yeah; and the haunting sound of my own thoughts that shouted, *"You were not so gentle yesterday."*

The day was *supposed* to be perfect. (*I know, my first mistake*). My kids were *supposed* to want to spend every waking moment at my side before they embarked on their adventures at camp. Forget the fact that they enjoyed the company of friends they brought along for our trip to the beach. They were *supposed* to understand my excessive, unrealistic expectations. Honestly, I didn't quite decipher them myself until I spent some time in prayer and reflection. The Holy Spirit gently extracted the root of my bitter words. This was the last family vacation before our daughter graduated from high school, and my unruly emotions put everyone in a pressure cooker.

I can quickly become demanding during demanding seasons. Days that are *supposed* to be joyful implode when I don't manage my feelings and reactions well. I become crabby, snippy, and harsh. That's when I start hunting for the remote. Trust me; regret tastes terrible.

Perhaps you, too, long for "do-over days." Although I'm far from perfect in this area, I sincerely want to glorify God and learn from my mistakes. Our words should drip with tenderness, yet too often they demolish trust. We don't have to allow the *"if only"* moments to run us over and ruin God's plans.

## LIFE MAY NOT PROVIDE US WITH A REMOTE CONTROL, BUT WE CAN STILL AVOID THE SOUR AFTERTASTE OF REGRET

**Evaluate expectations.** Prayerfully consider whether your expectations are healthy and realistic. Invite the Holy Spirit to guide you toward necessary adjustments in the attitudes of your heart and in the dynamics of your relationships.

**Expect the unexpected.** *"Blessed are the flexible for they shall not break."* Striving for perfection is a set-up for failure. It's noble to desire excellence and search for ways to squeeze the best out of every day. However, remember that things rarely go as planned. Keep a stellar attitude and stay adaptable.

**Exercise self-control.** Galatians Chapter 5 lists *"self-control"* as evidence of the Holy Spirit in our lives. God didn't dole out divine remote controls, but He does help us grow in His divine nature. Reach for self-control when things seem out of control and you'll never need a remote control. Look at 2 Peter 1:3–4:

> *"His divine power has given us everything we need for life and godliness through our knowledge of Him who called us by His own glory and goodness. Through these He has given us His very great and precious promises, so that through them you may participate in the divine nature and escape the corruption in the world caused by evil desires."*

**Examine your heart.** Rotten fruit reveals a rotten root. Allow the Holy Spirit to excavate places of your heart, pull up negative motives, and eradicate wrong attitudes. He's an expert in identifying the detrimental thought patterns that lurk behind destructive behaviors.

**Eat the Word.** We renew our mind with His truth by devouring the Word of God. Eat God's Word and you won't have to eat your own. Don't let the bitter taste of regret obscure God's purposes in your life. Life may not come with a remote control, but it does come with a manual: God's Word.

Peter, who wrote today's passage of Scripture, tasted regret on more than one occasion. Yet, as He allowed Jesus to teach him and the Holy Spirit to grow him, he learned how to do away with "do-over" days. Beautiful friends, we can, too.

**Astounded,**
*Angela*

# GOD'S FINGERPRINTS

*"And we all, who with unveiled faces contemplate the Lord's glory, are being transformed into his image with ever-increasing glory, which comes from the Lord, who is the Spirit."*

2 CORINTHIANS 3:18

Butterflies are a striking portrait of transformation. I am intrigued by their unusual beauty and ability to pollenate and decorate our world. Their delicate wings dance in the wind and remind us of God's infinite creativity. A caterpillar embraces the possibility of a new life as a butterfly as she spins a cocoon. While inside, her body completely dissolves and reforms. When the time is right, the cocoon splits down the middle. Tiny wings press into the open air and a lovely, entirely new creature emerges.

After a severe health crisis, a large scar now runs the length of my torso. I relate to each step of this amazing, God-ordained process. My journals are full of stories about butterflies God has sent my way, particularly on trips to Africa, reminding me of His love. I call these butterfly sightings, "God's fingerprints." While in West Africa, I needed hospitalization for a violent allergic reaction to something I ate. I spent the night in a bare hospital room in the most primitive of surroundings but slept on sheets covered with—yep, you guessed it—*butterflies*.

While ministering in Tanzania, I enjoyed a brief respite in between our hectic ministry schedule to safari in Ruaha National Game Park. My companion returned home due to the death of a family member. Although this is one of my favorite places on earth, staying by myself in a large tent without electricity or cell service is frightening. I tried my best to get a few hours of sleep while lions and elephants serenaded nearby. To add insult to injury, I ate something at dinner the second evening that prompted the same reaction in my body as whatever had landed me in the hospital years earlier. It was a tough night as I made numerous trips to the bathroom and longed for home. The next morning, while the team went on the last game drive, I stayed back to rest. They moved me to a tent closer to the main camp where I lay in a hammock and slept. Embellishing the hammock cloth was—yep, you guessed it—*butterflies*.

Transformation is not an effortless process, whether for a butterfly, or for us. But if we push through the difficulties we encounter, we experience supernatural joy. In 1 Samuel Chapter 1, we meet Hannah, a woman who experienced remarkable transformation. As you read her heart-wrenching story, you discover she desperately wanted a child. In the ancient world, motherhood was the aim of all married women, and life was hard for a childless woman. Distraught, Hannah poured out the anguish of her soul in prayers to God in the tabernacle at Shiloh. In thanksgiving for a son, Hannah offered to give him back in service to the Lord. God answered Hannah's prayer, and Samuel, the prophet-priest of Israel was born.

Perhaps she wrestled with the temptation to break her promise once she held Samuel in her arms. She loved her son, but she gave him over to the God who gave him to her. God's fingerprints were on her life. She weaned Samuel between three and five years of age and delivered him to the House of the Lord at Shiloh to begin his service to God under the care of Eli, the priest. God transformed her barrenness to joy, rewarding her with more children and a first-born son that faithfully served God his entire life, becoming one of the most beloved rulers in Israel.

I had the privilege of traveling to Shiloh, the very place where Hannah came thousands of years earlier to beseech God for a son. My breath caught in the back of my throat as I thought of the tears that wet the hallowed ground where I now stood. I reflected silently on the countless times God listened to the desperate cries of my heart. The God that met Hannah is the God that transforms us. He hears our cries and washes away our weariness.

**God's fingerprints are everywhere; you only need to look for them.** You don't have to travel to Israel to experience the supernatural touch of God on your life. Any moment can become your own personal Shiloh. Simply embrace transformation.

**Astounded,**

*Angela*

# LIFE IS WHAT WE MAKE IT

*"I always pray with joy because of your partnership in the gospel from the first day until now, being confident of this, that he who began a good work in you will carry it on to completion until the day of Christ Jesus."* PHILIPPIANS 1:6

It was every parent's worst nightmare.

Our family slathered on the sunscreen and bolted into Busch Gardens, eager to start our day of adventure. Instantly, our senses became overwhelmed by the spectacle of Clydesdale horses, the roar of a passing train, and the scent of funnel cake. Struggling with the map, I turned to ask an employee for directions. In the blink of an eye, he was gone. Our son, Christian, not more than six or seven years of age at the time, had continued walking, enticed by his new surroundings. My husband and I began to scream his name while our daughter, Gabrielle, clutched my hand. *"Christian! Christian!"* It was nearly impossible to find him in the sea of people crowded into the front entrance of the park. *And then, we spotted him.* The railroad tracks sign, lowered for the oncoming train, stopped him just thirty feet to our left. Relieved beyond measure, we scooped him up, took a deep breath and thanked God for His grace.

Those few seconds, filled with sheer panic, felt like an eternity. It's frightening to misplace something of value. If you've ever lost your way in the dark, lost your child in a store, or lost your wallet on an errand, you've experienced that sickening pit in your stomach. Yet, one of the most treasured things we can lose is our joy. Many of us walk through times when a sea of issues crowds in on us, leaving us frantically searching for joy. I wrote, *"Finding Joy When Life is Out of Focus: A Study of Philippians for Joy-Thirsty Women,"* as a resource encouraging us to look through the lens of God's perspective and love the life we see.

Scripture says that the joy of the Lord is our strength. Joy and happiness are not the same thing. Happiness could be defined as an attitude of satisfaction, based on our circumstance. Too often, we search for happiness through the fulfilment we receive from our job, financial status, or a relationship. This renders us victims to chance. Marriages become strained. Financial landscapes waver. Health deteriorates. Joy, on the other hand, is a choice. Life isn't the luck of the draw; life is what we make it. Joy is a gift from God to those who believe, produced in us by the Holy Spirit. Maybe, like me, you wrestle not so much with how to receive joy, but how to maintain it.

The word *joy* is mentioned more times in the four chapters of Philippians than anywhere else in Scripture. Philippians 1:1-6 shares the following:

*"Paul and Timothy, servants of Christ Jesus, To all God's holy people in Christ Jesus at Philippi, together with the overseers and deacons: Grace and peace to you from God our Father and the Lord Jesus Christ. I thank my God every time I remember you. In all my prayers for all of you, I always pray with joy because of your partnership in the gospel from the first day until now, being confident of this, that he who began a good work in you will carry it on to completion until the day of Christ Jesus."*

## THESE VERSES GIVE US FIVE KEYS TO CHOOSE JOY

- Rehearse the blessings of God instead of the offenses by others. (V. 3)
- Redirect your prayers for others instead of praying only for your own needs. (V. 4)
- Remember that you are not alone. Combat isolation by connecting with a friend or small group. (V. 5)
- Recognize God as your Source of dependency instead of focusing on people's deficiencies. (V. 6)
- Rebuild relationships instead of barriers. Give hope an open road.

Don't get lost when life becomes disorienting. We can find joy during seasons of adversity with one subtle shift: allowing God to focus our lens on His perspective. Choose an others-minded life steeped in joy. You'll discover more than your lost car keys; you'll find purpose.

**Astounded,**
*Angela*

# COFFEE SHOP
# CONVERSATION

*"Who do you say that I am?"*　　　　　MATTHEW 16:15

The chair squeaked across the wooden floor as he took a seat next to my husband, Dale. He leaned forward, placed his elbows on the table and clasped his fingers together. Those weathered hands cared for countless children during his years as a pediatrician. His tired eyes searched for subtle signs leading to many a diagnosis. Yet this morning, he searched for something else.

*"Do you have a minute, your holiness?"* he queried.

Dale felt a grin cross his face, the same way it had numerous times before. After so many similar mornings in the same coffee shop, he expected the familiar greeting. Some days he referred to Dale as "preacher," and other days, "priest." One morning, he merely crossed his chest as Dale walked by. Dale had given up explaining that he was not Catholic and embraced the affectionate titles donned by this colorful, casual acquaintance. His best guess was that his brilliant coffee shop friend was an agnostic. This morning felt different, and Dale shifted the weight of his attention to his query.

*"Sure. What's up?"*

*"Why believe in an unemployed Jew? Why would an unemployed Jew be the spokesperson for Christianity?"*

Dale slowly set his espresso on the table, and his gaze momentarily dropped. The questions both jarred and intrigued him.

*"Wow, I've never had anyone ask me that before. To tell you the truth, I don't know,"* Dale replied with brutal honesty.

*"That's the best answer anyone has ever given me. In all my years of asking, that's the most refreshing answer I could receive."* The man's shoulders relaxed as he sat back into the chair. Years of wondering and seeking washed over his face.

Dale wrestled with the magnitude of the moment. *"Listen, I can give you a lot of different theological answers, Scriptures and historical proof. But the bottom line? You have to accept Him by faith. I believe Jesus is Who He says He is. I've staked my life on it. By the way— He was a carpenter for thirty years and then focused on His ministry for the last three years. He was employed by His Dad."*

Dale decided to stop there. Although so much more could have been said, he didn't want to damage the relationship he attempted to build. A hug and a handshake later, the morning routine returned but the gravity of the conversation lingered.

That conversation cast a long shadow over my thoughts. I pondered the many possible reasons he hasn't taken the leap of faith. I wondered if he would ever visit our church. I considered stopping by the coffee shop myself to meet this interesting man and perhaps start my own dialogue.

Jesus never shrunk back from the "why" questions. He fielded questions from His disciples, Pilate, and Herod, just to name a few. Even John the Baptist, as he faced his darkest hour, wondered if Jesus was the Christ. Jesus can handle our "why" questions. But if you ask, be prepared for questions of His own. If Jesus was sitting in that coffee shop today, I have a feeling He might ask the same question of us that He asked 2000 years ago in Matthew 16:15: *"Who do you say that I am?"*

Jesus posed this crucial inquiry to His disciples in Caesarea Philippi. This notorious site was home to the gods of every nation carved into the side of a cliff. As I visited the site on my trip to Israel, I imagined the pivotal moment when Peter acknowledges Jesus as the Messiah. Every person on the planet has to answer that question. Was Jesus a prophet? Good man? Teacher? Yes, all of the above. But He is also the Son of God, the Savior of mankind, and Risen King. He alone is the Way, the Truth, and the Life. Until we settle that question in our hearts, nothing else matters.

In case you're wondering, he *did* come to church one Easter Sunday morning. The coffee shop eventually closed, and their paths never crossed again. But that moment made an impact. Keep your eyes open for your own "coffee shop" conversation this week. You just never know.

**Astounded,**

*Angela*

# A LETTER FROM A LONELY LAUNDRY BASKET

*"No one will be able to stand up against you all the days of your life. As I was with Moses, so I will be with you. I will never leave you nor forsake you."* JOSHUA 1:9

Dear Angela,

What did I do wrong? I've been faithful and dependable, haven't I? I graciously embraced your kids' stinky socks and favorite worn-out pajamas. I enjoyed my front row seat to their changing sizes and styles. I held it all together when I was overstuffed after youth camps or during college breaks. Some days we just hung out for hours while every bed got a fresh set of sheets or closets went through spring cleaning. I felt wanted...valued...needed. And then with no warning, nothing. Nada. Zip!

I anticipated, day after day, for that doorknob to turn. And I wondered: what did I do wrong? I hope this is just some kind of simple misunderstanding or oversight. I trust that next week will be different; we can get back to normal around here. Until then, I'll try to wait patiently and fight back the tears.

Lovingly,
*Your Lonely Laundry Basket*

Late one summer, our son enjoyed a week of vacation with a friend while our daughter moved back into her university apartment. The house was eerily quiet, and I didn't do a single load of laundry for days. *Not one.* I kept waiting for the laundry basket to fill up enough to warrant running the washing machine. When it finally did, it was a pitiful half a load. You'd think I would welcome a stretch without piles of laundry. But as I walked past that door each day, the lump in my throat got bigger and my laundry basket got lonelier.

It's not just about the laundry basket: they're adulting and I'm adapting. The only normal thing about it is that nothing is normal. I stumble through some days with a profound sense of loss. Perhaps you're experiencing your own change of season and your "normal" has shifted. Shifted from bassinet to big bed. Carpool to quiet. Bustling to boredom. Perhaps you're struggling to climb into a cold bed every night after the loss of your spouse. Perhaps you've stored your hairbrush in a dusty drawer after the loss of your hair to cancer. Or perhaps you're staring at an empty calendar and a blank checkbook after the loss of a job. When something shifts our normal, we can find ourselves struggling with change. Finding a new normal can be particularly difficult when change comes without warning.

Joshua, Chapter 1 shines center spotlight on a man struggling with monumental loss and a shifted normal. After the death of his mentor and leader, Moses, God appoints Joshua to take the Israelites into the promised land. God's instructions to Joshua give us a glimpse into his emotional state. Five times in three verses, God commands Joshua to be strong and courageous. But before God gives the commands, He gives a promise:

> "No one will be able to stand up against you all the days of your life. As I was with Moses, so I will be with you. I will never leave you nor forsake you,"　　　　　　　　　　　　　　JOSHUA 1:9

God knows the condition of our fragile hearts when we stare down the unfamiliar landscape of a shifted normal. I don't have all the answers. I'm navigating my own new normal as we speak. But I have discovered three keys to living with a lonely laundry basket and an altered normal:

- Release disappointment and trust your emotions to God. Talk it out so it doesn't take you out.
- Remember precious moments and reinvest your gifts and talents in new areas. Try that new venture you put off for a rainy day.
- Relinquish control and stay open to innovative ways God wants to use this season.

God lovingly applies healing balm to the wounds left by deep loss. He strengthens our hearts by revealing unexpected opportunities as we refocus our energies. It's okay if your laundry basket sees a little less use. You're still needed and valued. Just like Joshua, we are not doing this alone. Be strong and courageous! God is with you every step of the way.

**Astounded,**

*Angela*

# HAND GOD THE CAR KEYS

*"Show me your ways, Lord, teach me your paths. Guide me in your truth and teach me, for you are God my Savior, and my hope is in you all day long."* PSALM 25:4-5

Put me on a plane, a boat, or a train, and I promise one thing: I'll get motion sick. Travel plans make Dramamine my new best friend. I wasn't always this way. Perhaps it's a lovely ailment that comes with age. Whatever the reason, it's annoying. However, I can sleep off motion sickness far quicker than I can recover from the learning curves of life.

When I transitioned out of a twenty-year ministry role and into a different one, I weathered a year of twists and turns. I traversed unfamiliar landscapes and developed new organizational systems. I struggled to manage the sharp learning curves of life without sliding into the ditch. I felt incompetent and insecure, wondering at times if anything I did made a difference. Change can be tough; especially when it requires a hefty amount of adjustment. Maybe you can relate to the learning curve change brings.

- A change in your address and the pull of strange surroundings ...
- A change in your family dynamics and a quiet house...
- A change in your body and unwelcome limitations ...

In the middle of that challenging season, God spoke these words into my spirit: *"You're not the driver."* In other words, Angela, I'm in control of this ride—not you. Ouch. At first, I felt chastised and nervous. After all, I'm even more nauseated when I'm not driving...when I'm not in control. Yet, when the roads of life become risky, the safest place is in the passenger's seat. He reassured my anxious heart with these words:

*"I know it's been a tough year. Let Me lead; let Me drive. I know when to brake and when to accelerate. I know when to pull over and when to stop. You can rest in that and trust Me to handle anything the road of life may bring. I'm not going to let you slide into the ditch. Trust Me. Hand me the car keys."*

David, the shepherd boy, songwriter, warrior and King, navigated learning curves of his own. He even slid off the road a few times, towed back out by God's mercy. His words in Psalm 25:4-5 teach us to remain dependent on God during seasons of change.

*"Show me your ways, Lord, teach me your paths. Guide me in your truth and teach me, for you are God my Savior, and my hope is in you all day long."*

Just as God promised to be faithful to David, He promises to lead us. He will show us, guide us, and teach us. We can place our hope in Him—all day long. Isn't it a relief to know we don't have to figure all this out alone? God longs to show us His ways if we'll let Him put the coordinates into the GPS. Maybe a curve took you out and you need the grace of God to pull you to safety. No matter what stretch of road you're navigating, find hope in the same words that steadied my fragile heart: *"You're not the driver."*

## TUCK THESE PRINCIPLES INTO YOUR GLOVE COMPARTMENT WHEN YOU TRAVEL THE ROAD OF CHANGE

- Slide on into the passenger's seat and let God drive.
- Ask for directions from your Guide.
- Slow down and pay close attention to your surroundings.
- Balance the curves of fresh growth with the flat road of familiar ground.
- Pull over to rest and refill your tank through personal Sabbath.

Go ahead, hand God the car keys to your life. Because when He's in control, it's an amazing ride.

**Astounded,**
*Angela*

# WHEN TO KEEP YOUR MOUTH SHUT

*"Those who guard their mouths and their tongues keep themselves from calamity."*                                     PROVERBS 21:23

When I first saw her, I cringed. Hair dye gone bad…leathery skin from far too many exposures to a tanning bed…white strapless top meant for someone half her age. She complimented every bite of her meal with audible commentary.

*"This sauce. This cheese. It's just fantastic!"* she quipped to the waiter. *"Could I have another glass of wine?"*

Great, I thought. Here I am trying to enjoy a dinner out with my hubby to celebrate our anniversary, and there's a third wheel. A loud, attention-seeking, slightly inebriated wheel. She stared blankly out the large front window of the restaurant at the passersby on the downtown street. Against the backdrop of misty rain and overcast skies, the loneliness was palpable.

*"She reminds me of the Beatles song,"* I haphazardly spoke into the air.

*"Which one?"* my husband inquired.

*"You know...the one where she leaves her face in a jar by the door..."* my voice trailed off as I let the moment sink in.

*"Stop staring,"* my husband scolded.

Honestly, I didn't realize I was. I was just, I don't know, uncomfortable. And slightly annoyed. My mind struggled to focus as I re-read the menu a few times.

*Ugh, I thought. She's ordering dessert. She's getting louder and more obnoxious with every course.*

*"Honey, what are you ordering? Come on."* My husband's voice grew stern as I struggled to redirect my energies off of the lonely-hearts club woman and onto my husband. I bristled at her awkward attempts to start conversations with waiters on the other side of the room.

I fumbled for my phone to text my daughter. *"This lady is in here by herself in a strapless shirt and she's too old for it and weird and drinking too much and talking to herself at the top of her lungs."*

And I was close. Close to saying something.

**Perhaps someone should tell her she's had enough. Maybe I should let my waiter know that she's disturbing our anniversary dinner.**

And then I just got sad. Really, really sad, that someone was so conspicuously lonely. The sting of shame flushed my face as I watched our waiter serve her.

*Hmmm, they seem awfully jovial. Maybe she comes here a lot.*

*"Here, wrap up this dessert,"* she glibly barked at him.

*"Don't you want to finish it?"* he asked.

*"No, you take it home. I don't want all that sugar in my house."*

**Take it home? Why are you asking your waiter to take it home?**

My jumbled thoughts fought for order as he brought back her check.

*"Thanks for coming in tonight, Mom. It was great to see you."*

**Mom?? Mom. This woman is his mom. She came to sit and be with her son. She came to enjoy a meal at the place he works and convey the joy she savored in every bite. She came to not be alone.**

*"Oh my word, Dale. She's his mom. Thank GOD I didn't say anything to him."*

I picked up my phone and slowly texted my daughter back. *"We just realized this lady is the waiter's mom. Thank God I didn't say anything. She was here by herself to support her son."*

*"Yeah, exactly. You never, never know."*

*"I'm going to write about this, Gab. When to keep your mouth shut."*

Lesson learned over paella and scallops. Who am I to judge... to have a word with the manager...to apologize to the waiter for the unruly behavior of a patron? Who am I to allow my quest for an uninterrupted evening blur my vision of someone else's pain? Who am I to speak when I need to keep my mouth shut? I shudder at the thought of what that gentle, 20-ish-year-old waiter might have felt had I said something not-so-nice about his mom. I have a lump in my throat just thinking about it. I don't know her story, but tonight she was written into mine.

God wants us to see more than leathery skin and hollow eyes. We need to see a mom. A son. A story that's worth telling because it's a story God is writing. That anniversary is one for the books, not because of a spectacular view, but because I saw a mom and a son, and my not-so-flattering reflection in their mirror. Let's learn to keep our mouths shut and our hearts open.

**Astounded,**

*Angela*

# AN IMPERFECT MESS

*"All who are hunting for you, oh let them sing and be happy. Let those who know what you're all about tell the world You're great and not quitting. And me? I'm a mess. I'm nothing and I have nothing: make something out of me. You can do it, God."*

PSALM 40:16-17

I would love to tell you that I have it all together every day. But, some days, I'm a mess. I struggled to balance ministry roles and parenting two teenagers. I watched countless cooking shows, yet rarely tried one of the recipes. I take group fitness classes and still come home and indulge in chips and dip. I call myself a recovering perfectionist, determined to make peace with my shortcomings. Part of it stems from unrealistic expectations of myself and my tendency toward an overscheduled calendar. But before I allow that line of reasoning to justify a pity-party, I remember life-altering words spoken to me by my piano teacher, Dr. June Kean.

She was my mentor, my teacher, and my friend. I lost her several years ago to brain cancer. She may have been the most influential person in my life. I was fortunate to be among a handful of high school students she taught alongside her college students. She coached me through Evangel University where I graduated with a Music Education Degree in Piano and Voice. Her office was an imperfect mess, her influence, unparalleled. I carry distinct sounds and unforgettable images as treasured memories...

*Countless covers... Rachmaninoff, Chopin, Bach, Beethoven... scattered across her office.*

*Arrangements for Fine Arts competitions written on lip-stick stained napkins.*

*A surplus of pencils to mark missed tempos and dreadful key signatures.*

*Feet that played the pipe organ like nobody's business and walked with integrity.*

*Hands that reached far beyond an octave and words that reached deep into my life.*

She could guess within a half hour how much I practiced during the week. The imperfect mess I am, it was usually less time than she required. Excuses filled the air as I regaled her with dramatic stories to distract from my inadequacies. Perhaps weary from this dance, she calmly and deliberately countered back during a lesson:

*"Angela, you will always have a crisis in life. You need to decide: are you going to live from crisis to crisis?"*

The words simultaneously stung and resonated to my core.

*"No,"* I thought to myself. *"That is not how I want to live."*

She loved me, mess and all. Although I can't say I've never had another messy moment, I can say that her words stuck to my soul. We will always have a crisis in life, big ones, like cancer and family chaos, and small ones like over-used recipes and calendar conflicts. What do we do with our imperfect mess?

How I wish I could call my mentor and garner her advice. I miss her. Yet, I have a Heavenly Father that loves me, perfectly, despite my imperfect mess. He invites me to sit down with Him and regale Him with my drama. Sometimes He corrects, and sometimes He encourages. But, He always reminds me that He is perfect so I don't have to be.

I'm heartened by the words of Psalm 40:16-18 in the Message:

*"All who are hunting for you, oh let them sing and be happy. Let those who know what you're all about tell the world You're great and not quitting. And me? I'm a mess. I'm nothing and I have nothing: make something out of me. You can do it, God."*

What do we do with our imperfect mess? We yield it to God and ask Him to make something beautiful out of us. We are loved unconditionally by a perfect God. So, go ahead, pass me the chips and dip, please. You know what I think? Dr. June Kean and my Heavenly Father are smiling.

**Astounded,**

*Angela*

# WHISTLES AND WITNESS

*"For I am not ashamed of the Gospel, because it is the power of God that brings salvation to everyone that believes."*

ROMANS 1:16

After eight hours on an overnight flight in cramped conditions, the Amsterdam Airport provided a welcome respite to stretch my legs and refuel. Green with envy at the business class travelers and groggy from lack of sleep, I ordered up a mouth-watering plate of eggs stuffed with cheese and bacon, fresh orange juice, and a strong cappuccino. I snatched a comfy table where my dad and I could relax for a bit before we boarded the next, long trek into Dar Es Salaam, Tanzania. This once-in-a-lifetime father-daughter trip, a couple years in the making, had only just begun.

*"Would he love Africa as much as I do?"* I wondered. *"Would the people of Africa find a home in his heart as they had mine?"* The

familiar melody of my dad's distinct whistle interrupted my thoughts. As he ordered his breakfast from the European cashier he just met, I observed from a distance.

*"I heard you say, 'God bless you' to your other patrons,"* my dad commented with optimism. *"Are you a Christian?"*

*"Yes, I am,"* the tall, slender, blonde gentleman replied.

*"Great! So, you've made Jesus your Lord?"* my Dad inquired.

*"Yes, I have."*

I felt a small, sheepish smile form across my face, and I knew. I knew this conversation was destined to repeat many times throughout the next two weeks. My dad sees the world through a singular lens: *"Do you know Jesus?"* If I'm honest, I must admit to the many things that blur the lens through which I see my world. *Understandable* things. *Realistic* things. *Practical* things. Things we all relate to…

**Like fatigue.** After all, it's 4 o'clock in-the-morning for my body. I'm too fatigued to notice a cashier's kind tone and generous spirit. And I feel…*ashamed.*

**Like focus.** I'm preoccupied by my breakfast order and quest to exchange dollars to euros. I'm too focused on the incosequential to see the need right in front of me. And I feel…*ashamed.*

**Like fear.** I'm worried that people will…will what? Laugh? Scoff? Become agitated with me? My inability to pinpoint any genuine cause for fear makes me feel…*ashamed.*

**Like faith.** After all, maybe this peppy cashier doesn't want to discuss faith over strawberries and omelets while weary travelers wait in line to place their order. Isn't faith, you know, a personal thing? And I feel…*ashamed.*

*"Do you know Jesus?"* Across three continents and multiple settings, my dad's caring conversation, gentle probing, and sincere interest remained on display. Over and over, he whistled,

and he witnessed. Whistled and witnessed. It seemed nothing could take his whistle or deter his witness...

*With passengers on planes.*

*With staff of hotels.*

*With vendors in the market.*

*With students at a school.*

*With a Muslim guide in a National Park.*

*With a waitress named "Neema" in our Hotel in Dar, as he explains the meaning of her name, "Grace."*

And you know what? The Muslim guide asked for a Swahili Bible. Neema came to church. Who knows what other seeds were sown this side of eternity? Romans 1:16 began to ruminate in my spirit throughout these two weeks with my Dad.

*"For I am not ashamed of the Gospel, because it is the power of God that brings salvation to everyone that believes."*

In Rome, the center of the known world at the time, Paul boldly declared his stand. He firmly grasped a simple truth: we are all in need of salvation. God is willing to save. Am I willing to witness? The realities of my life demand I stop and reflect honestly on this question: *"Am I ashamed of the Gospel?"*

If I'm going to be *fatigued*, let it be that I have worn myself out sharing the Gospel. If I'm going to be *focused*, let it be on those who don't know Christ. If I'm going to *fear*, may it be that I might miss a chance to demonstrate the love of Jesus. If I'm going to be a person of *faith*, may I truly believe the Gospel has power. I can't whistle, not even a little bit. But I can witness. Will you join me?

**Astounded,**

*Angela*

# PERHAPS CAPTAIN HOOK WAS RIGHT

*"Therefore, since we are surrounded by such a great cloud of witnesses, let us throw off everything that hinders and the sin that so easily entangles. And let us run with perseverance the race marked out for us, fixing our eyes on Jesus, the pioneer and perfecter of faith."* HEBREWS 12:1-2

You can't tame it. You can't get it back once it's gone. And, under no circumstances can you make it stop. Perhaps Captain Hook was right about that dreaded crocodile: time. While playing the piano for one of my daughter's many musical theatre shows, *Peter Pan*, I pondered Hook's consternation over the crocodile which swallowed both his hand and a clock. The "tick-tock" announced his arrival, to Hook's dismay. The lesson of the symbolism in the beloved story? Try as we may, we can't outrun time.

The summer my daughter prepared to leave for college, I stopped counting the days and started measuring the minutes. Don't get me wrong. I was thrilled to watch her launch into a new chapter of her life. But it was hard. In the moments leading up to my son telling his sister good-bye, I felt sick. Nauseated. Hot. Dizzy. *Sideways.* Some seasons of life feel that way. *Up* seems *down* and we feel askew.

Did I wish I could go back? Do some things over? Sure. Some days.

Did I wonder if I did enough? Sure. Most days.

Did I worry if she would be okay, get enough sleep, and carve out a new life? Sure. Just about every day.

Our daughter graduated from college and began her professional career as a performer. One key lesson I learned during that period was to treasure each day like it might be our last. Sideways seasons invite us to grow in our dependency on God. They can also teach us to avoid regret by stewarding our time well. As we lean into His Word, He faithfully strengthens us with the grace we need. Hebrews 12:1-2 provides us with four keys to honor healthy boundaries when it comes to the gift of time.

> *"Therefore, since we are surrounded by such a great cloud of witnesses, let us throw off everything that hinders and the sin that so easily entangles. And let us run with perseverance the race marked out for us, fixing our eyes on Jesus, the pioneer and perfecter of faith."*

**Sidestep hurdles that hinder.** Throw off everything that threatens to impede God's will. Distraction and procrastination create obstacles to progress. Even good things can rob of us God's best and prevent us from the wise use of our time. Discipline your schedule by asking the Holy Spirit, *"Is this a good thing, or a God-thing?"* He will lead you.

**Avoid getting tangled up.** Nothing will steal your time faster than sin. The writer of Hebrews reminds us that sin *easily* entangles. God established principles in His Word for our benefit. When we entertain sin of any kind—jealousy, bitterness, immorality, or dishonesty, just to name a few—we become ensnared and ineffective. Thankfully, God made a way for us! Forgiveness and a fresh start are a prayer away.

**Keep moving forward.** Trials and adversity provide fertile ground for the enemy to sow lies. Don't become derailed by deception or become sidelined by the enemy's schemes. Keep moving forward with truth and run the race before you.

**Fix our eyes on Jesus.** While climbing Mt. Kilimanjaro in 2011, I hit a wall on the fifth day due to severe altitude sickness. I honestly didn't think I could take another step. A guide got in front of me and uttered these simple words, *"Follow my steps. Follow my pace."* He led me up that steep incline to my personal summit at 16,000 feet. Jesus is your pacesetter. Don't selfishly run ahead of Him, or aimlessly lag behind. Keep your eyes on our Guide, Jesus, every step of the way.

Invest your time in people and endeavors that hold eternal value. Perhaps Captain Hook was right; time might just be the most precious commodity we have. Let's spend it wisely.

**Astounded,**
*Angela*

# DISCOVER BEAUTY IN UNEXPECTED PLACES

*"For God so loved the world that He gave His only Son; that whosoever believes in Him should not perish but have everlasting life."*

JOHN 3:16

Americans will spend more than *450* billion dollars on purchases that accompany the Christmas season. We go to great lengths to find the perfect gift: take laps around the mall, scroll through the monstrosity of Amazon, or alas, pick up the last-minute Starbucks gift card. Some of us smother our precious cargo with Styrofoam peanuts and ship packages across the country to friends and family. Still others buy stock in double-stick tape as we patiently wrap must-have electronics and eye-shadow palettes.

We exchange cheesy white-elephant packages at office parties and deliver frosting-slathered sugar cookies to our neighbors. We donate Barbie dolls to the local toy drives, drop our change in buckets to bell ringing Santas, and offer crayon masterpieces to our kids' teachers. Gifts, gifts, and more gifts.

And then, just like that, the flurry of holiday festivities is over. You know the scene. Carefully crafted wrapping paper lies in a crumpled mound on the living room floor. That horrid orange sweater heads into the return pile while the last crumb of yummy goodness heads to our hips. We're pooped. Mom and Dad savor a much-needed break, teachers relish the peace and quiet, and office computer screens sit blank for a couple days.

I'm not sure when the concept of gift giving began but let's be honest—we all love to give and receive gifts. On a trip to the Holy Land, my Christmas gift came early one year in a little town called Bethlehem.

*Beauty is still found in the most unexpected places.* Nowhere is this truer than in the walled city of Bethlehem. Surrounded by armed guards and under Palestinian rule, I struggled to picture ancient streets where a young couple named Mary and Joseph stopped to find respite. It was here God gave the greatest gift: *grace intersected humanity.*

I found myself drawn to every word from our Christian guide. I bent low at the Door of Humility to enter the world's oldest church, The Church of the Nativity. All bow to visit the birthplace of the King of Kings. Amidst the pungent smell of burning incense and the cacophony of Greek Orthodox prayers, God met me in a deeply personal way. For the first time in far too long, I sensed the magnitude of God's divinely orchestrated symphony. I felt a dizzying awareness that God chose to include my story in the fabric of His story, written before time began.

I felt tiny. Humbled. Overwhelmed.

God's plan was to redeem mankind by sending His Son to be born, not in the majesty of a palace, but in a dark, damp cave used as a stable. *Beauty is still found in the most unexpected places.*

Bethlehem is home to a unique store with some of the most splendid Nativity sets found anywhere in the world. Living bravely behind a wall, local Christian artisans carve exquisite pieces out of olive wood. Resilient, they refuse to be diminished by brokenness. Although my budget would not allow me to take a Nativity home, I still received a gift: the indelible imprints on my heart from the unexpected beauty of Bethlehem.

What if the best present isn't found in a mall or an online behemoth? More than anything, let's give the gift of beauty. Let's refuse to be diminished by brokenness and carve beauty into our world.

*Our neighbors. Our family. Our schools.*

*The lost. The hurting. The fractured.*

*Beauty is still found in the most unexpected places.*

Grace intersects humanity when you choose a posture of availability. Let humility invite you to bow low and encounter God in a new way. And as you do, let wonder wash over you once again.

**Astounded,**

*Angela*

# IF MY SANDALS COULD SPEAK

*"How beautiful on the mountains are the feet of those who bring good news, who proclaim peace, who bring good tidings, who proclaim salvation, who say to Zion, Your God reigns!"*

ISAIAH 52:7

Well, it finally happened. I guess deep down I always knew this day would come. My faithful pink and white Crocs, sandals I took on *every* trip to Africa, finally gave out. Ironically enough, after all I put them through in a decade of use, they simply split walking around my kitchen. As my heart flooded with emotion, I may or may not have resembled Tom Hanks character in *Cast Away*, undone by the loss of his trusty friend, "Wilson" the volleyball, to the ocean. Ahem.

I threw my sturdy sidekicks away, only to pillage through the trash to recover them. All that these Crocs have seen, heard, and experienced proved too much to send them to the dump. I sighed these words to my son: *"If these sandals could talk, wow... the stories they would tell."*

## IF MY CROCS COULD SHARE THEIR LIFE STORY, IT MIGHT SOUND SOMETHING LIKE THIS...

"How can I possibly sum up ten years' worth of memories in a few short paragraphs? I carried Angela into Ghana, Liberia, Tanzania, Malawi, and Kenya, and that's just on the African continent. In the Holy Land, I walked where Jesus walked and stepped into the Jordan River. I served as Angela's companion on family vacations to sandy beaches and Smokey Mountain cabins. I traveled through more airports than I can remember. But once the red clay of Africa embedded herself into my treads, I knew I would never be the same.

I first touched down on African soil in 2007. Since then, Angela and I have made more than fifteen trips to the continent she loves so much. Every day of every journey was an adventure. I stood on makeshift soccer fields where boys kicked a ball they'd made out of twine. I strolled across real soccer fields preparing for open air crusades to share the Gospel in Daboya, Ghana. I witnessed thousands upon thousands of people make the arduous trek in their own worn sandals, to hear the Gospel shared by Evangelists Reinhard Bonnke and Daniel Kolenda in Liberia.

I stood in schools where hundreds of women from across Northern Ghana crowded to hear life-giving messages. I danced in a tambourine circle at one of those services. I visited orphanages that broke Angela's heart and celebrated the dedication of Haven of Hope, a home Angela helped to build for widowed pastors' wives and orphaned children in Malawi. I walked dusty roads in remote areas to meet the faces of women with ideas—who simply needed a place to start.

I held Angela up as she shared gospel illusions and Biblical stories with thousands of children at Kids Camps. I let her cover me with glitter and paint from more craft activities than I can count. I knelt with her in the huts of African chiefs and laid gently next to her cot as she slept in a mud hut. I was her bedside friend as she lay ill in a hospital bed. I marched across flooded streets as she resolved to make it to Soboba to visit a community she had blessed financially. I remember how the children greeted us with chants of, *"You are welcome, you are welcome."*

I dug through muddy village streets as she went to a late-night church service as village members braved torrential rain to thank her for donating chairs. I was gently washed off by a young boy as Angela stood on the muddy riverbank where both children and cows drank from the same water. I stood in corn fields where pastors had planted life-preserving crops from funds. I walked across swinging bridges and through the hallowed halls of slave castles. I watched thousands of women stand for hours in the pitch black to hear Angela share a message when the electricity went out in an outdoor conference.

I stepped into jeeps and felt the tall grass of the Ruaha Game Reserve as Angela rested. I moved Angela through Bible college campuses, including a week she and her father ministered side by side in Tanzania. I made the trip to Mt. Kilimanjaro and waited at the base as she climbed in her hiking boots. I held her as she crouched down next to Maasai women selling wares and village elders presenting Angela with chickens they killed for our meal. I rode in countless vehicles across the African countryside, stopping occasionally for bananas on the side of the road.

I struggled to hold her up as children in villages mobbed her as she handed out candy. I was nearly carried off by an unexpected rainstorm flooding the market as Angela rushed to get out. I stood in churches as Angela prepared to speak or lead worship. I helped her into a canoe as she crossed the river to get back to Daboya where they planted a church. I've seen the inside of tents, the ceramic tiles of guest homes, the halls of hotels and the mud floors of huts. I've listened to women's stories of heartbreak and faith. I've bent in two as Angela sat cross-legged in the dirt to tell a child about Jesus under an African tree.

I've been washed with spickets and hoses and buckets and water bottles, and even muddy water drawn from the river. But Angela's tears have washed me the most. We've been through a lot together; shared more memories than most people do across ten lifetimes. And maybe, even though I can't carry her another step, maybe she'll carry me in her suitcase, just to see where God will take us next."

*"How beautiful on the mountains are the feet of those who bring good news, who proclaim peace, who bring good tidings, who proclaim salvation, who say to Zion, Your God reigns!"*

ISAIAH 52:7

You, beautiful friend, were created to tell God's story.

**Astounded,**

*Angela*

# THE ONE THING GUARANTEED TO KILL YOUR CONFIDENCE

*"Each one should test their own actions. Then they can take pride in themselves alone, without comparing themselves to someone else."*                    GALATIANS 6:4

*"I'm the oldest one, here. Again. I don't even know why I'm doing this. I should just leave."* My fingers moved nervously across my iPhone keypad to text my daughter as my eyes darted anxiously across the crowded room, filled with perky twenty-somethings.

*"Mom, you'll be amazing!"* she texted back.

*"I'm probably not even what they're looking for."* My mind raced furiously, flooding my body with adrenaline.

*"You're prepared, Angela,"* I told myself. *"And if nothing else, you're rocking these turquoise blue heels."*

At 48 whopping years of age, I decided to audition for musical theater. I directed, wrote and accompanied more plays and musicals than I can count. But performing in them? Welllll, let's just say the last year I auditioned for one might start with 19 and end with 85. *Ahem.*

My daughter graduated from high school in the same year I transitioned out of leading worship. I realized that for the first time in many years, I had the chance to pursue new avenues of musical expression. I began taking voice lessons after a twenty-year hiatus. I sent out resumes and headshots and landed a few callbacks. It's quite a different experience than holding your daughter's ponytail holder while *she* tackles her own dizzying maze of auditions. I thrive on challenge and crave adventure, so I enjoyed this new season. But I'll be honest; I didn't plan for the level of insecurity and self-doubt that crept in like a thief.

There I was, sitting in the downstairs level of a health food store, waiting my turn for another audition. And right on cue, feelings of uncertainty and inadequacy made their grand entrance. My daughter's encouragement and my positive self-talk didn't seem to matter. Looking around at a room full of younger girls, I felt, well, old. A has-been. A somewhat tarnished version of my former self. And none of those girls had to even say a word; my own insecurities did the dirty work for them.

You may have no intention of finding your way to a musical theatre audition room (and can I just say I don't blame you.) But perhaps you're facing a new challenge or season, laced with self-doubt. Comparison is the one thing guaranteed to kill your confidence and keep you from God's best in your life.

## COMPARISON KILLS CONFIDENCE

Galatians 6:4 encourages us that,

> *"Each one should test their own actions. Then they can take pride in themselves alone, without comparing themselves to someone else."*

Comparison drives us deeper into insecurity and shifts our eyes onto ourselves, especially our flaws. It causes us to see others as a threat to our own happiness, blocking our ability to love generously. When we become self-conscious, we begin to miss what God wants to do through us. Insecurity makes it difficult to live an others-minded life.

As I paced outside that audition room, I noticed a chalkboard covered with a rainbow of chalk and personal sentiments. My eyes fell on a simple phrase and I felt as though God literally whispered these words into my ear:

> *"A flower does not think of competing to another flower next to it. It just blooms."*

Ahhhhh. I took a deep breath and felt my heart rate slow to a manageable pace. God reminds us that we don't have to be crippled by competition and comparison. He created us each with unique talents and gifts. He simply wants us to bloom.

I love walking through new doors to play, arrange, and perform in musical theatre. But that's only part of the point. God wants us to learn to depend on Him in entirely new ways when we stare down the opponent called insecurity. He will teach us to redirect our focus off comparison and onto confidence in Him. Ground your confidence in Christ and remember this: You don't need to be anyone else. You simply need to bloom.

**Astounded,**

*Angela*

# STAY JOYFUL IN SEASONS OF SUFFERING

*"But rejoice insofar as you share Christ's sufferings, that you may also rejoice and be glad when his glory is revealed."* 1 PETER 4:13

Shrouded by the cover of darkness, Peter crouched by the crackling fire. Only moments earlier, he swore his uncompromising devotion to Jesus. Yet, in the blur of Jesus' arrest, Peter ran, terrified at the prospect of suffering for the name of Christ. Restored by grace and commissioned to do great things for the kingdom, Peter penned 1 Peter Chapter 4 with a transformed perspective.

Under Emperor Nero's orders, the Roman governors prosecuted Christians as criminals. Peter encouraged the beleaguered believers scattered across Asia Minor to stand strong in the face of persecution. The threat of imprisonment and martyrdom loomed large, and Peter, himself, was eventually executed under Nero's cruel reign. The instructions in 1 Peter 4:12-19 serve as a template for the 21ˢᵗ century church undergoing persecution for the gospel today.

**Don't be surprised.** *"Beloved, do not be surprised at the fiery trial when it comes upon you to test you, as though something strange were happening to you."* (V. 12) God uses seasons of suffering to teach us obedience, steer us toward surrender, and bring glory to Himself.

**Suffering shouldn't surprise us; it should refine us.** Our attitude in times of testing determines the fruit of a trial. Verse 13 heartens us: *"But rejoice insofar as you share Christ's suffering that you may also rejoice and be glad when his glory is revealed."* We share not only in Christ's glory, but also in His sufferings. When I go through difficult situations, I'm tempted to huff, "Why me?" or lament "Woe is me." Peter's words challenge me to instead, prayerfully respond by seeking to understand how God can best use seasons of suffering to advance His kingdom.

**Don't be ashamed.** Verse 14 shares the promise of blessing in times of testing. *"If you are insulted for the name of Christ, you are blessed because the Spirit of glory and of God rests upon you."* When we endure persecution for our stand for righteousness, not because of our own wrongdoing, we experience the presence of the Holy Spirit in a unique way to empower us, embolden us, enable us and equip us. *"Yet if anyone suffers as a Christian, let him not be ashamed, but let him glorify God in that name."*

And Verses 17-18 beg us to sit with this truth: we may undergo hardship temporarily for our faith, but it's nothing compared to suffering for eternity for our lack of it. When our perspective is eternal, our suffering has purpose.

**Don't be derailed.** *"Therefore, let those who suffer according to God's will entrust their souls to a faithful Creator while doing good."* (V. 19). We can trust God to use seasons of suffering to bring us closer to Jesus and more dependent on Him. Nothing should deter us from our readiness to serve—joyfully—as Christ's representatives, or derail us from our God-given purpose. We don't have to let the fear of man or the intimidation of God's assignments keep us from obeying His call. The safest place we will ever be is in the center of God's will.

As I visit and minister in parts of the world deeply scarred by persecution, I become increasingly aware of my own sheltered experience. It's not that I haven't suffered. I survived debilitating health conditions that nearly took my life. As I wrestled with questions and struggled at times to fully trust Jesus, His love continually sustained and strengthened me. I still can't help but wonder if the western church truly grasps the message of Peter's words. Yet, the beauty of the Gospel is that in *whatever* way we take a stand for the Gospel, Christ is honored.

**Astounded,**
*Angela*

# FEARLESS FAITH

*"By faith the prostitute Rahab, because she welcomed the spies, was not killed with those who were disobedient."*   HEBREWS 11:31

Rahab brushed her long, chestnut-brown hair and pulled it taut at the nape of her neck. She tied it firmly with a crimson ribbon of fabric and felt her shoulders twinge from holding so much tension. Her hands dropped heavy into her lap as her frame exhaled deeply. She closed her eyes and allowed herself to imagine what it might be like to be somewhere else…any place where she mattered.

She couldn't remember the last time she wasn't tired. It was bad enough to be trapped inside a city where no one could move in or out. But she knew it was her own choices that entombed her most. She pressed her hand against the door, built against the city wall. *"So close yet impossible,"* she thought with resignation. She longed for a fresh start and wondered if a conversation she overheard just days before might hold the answer.

*"We must remain vigilant. We have enough supplies to last through a siege, even if it goes on for a couple of months. With what the Israelites have done to our neighbors, we can't risk them infiltrating our city. And after their escape through the Red Sea, who knows what could happen? The ban stays. No one goes in, no one goes out."*

The tremor in the men's voices exposed their fear, but something inside of her leapt at the possibilities. Could this be her chance for a clean slate?

Moses led God's people for 40 years through the wilderness, but Joshua took them across the Jordan River to possess the land given to them by God. First, they had to conquer Jericho—a critical, heavily fortified city and the key to all the land west of the Jordan.

They sent spies ahead to see what they faced. These men met a woman carrying a painful past and an uncertain future. They discovered the prostitute, Rahab, the unlikeliest of heroes with uncommon faith. She was stuck—in a sinful lifestyle, and in a wicked place, both set for destruction. Rahab dreamt of a different life; one where her worth was defined by what God said about her, not by the world. She put herself in grave danger to help the Israelites and God honored her obedience.

While in Israel, I filmed a video resource for my second Bible Study, *"Fearless: Ordinary Women of the Bible who Dared to do Extraordinary Things."* I sat mere feet from the only structure that remained when the walls of Jericho collapsed. As the brutal noonday sun beat across my face, one simple fact arrested my thoughts: a house built strategically against the town wall stood when the walls fell. Yet, even more incredulous, one woman, under the intense heat of pressure and her back against the wall, refused to bow to fear.

Rahab wanted out of this place.

She devised a plan, not out of selfishness, but out of authentic faith. The sign of her willingness and complete cooperation was a scarlet cord, hanging conspicuously in her window. No matter how strong the enemy looked on the outside, her faith remained intact on the inside. I'm so challenged by the courage of Rahab. It's much easier to just blend in with the crowd than to stand up for what is right.

**Our past doesn't have to paralyze our future.** You can get out from under anything that's trying to bury you. When you encounter Christ, you are freed from the identity put on you by the world. Grace is the undoing of something old and the unfolding of something new. It is the awareness that God picks us up out of the rubble and leads us to safety. It is the realization that God longs to save us, redeem us, and use us. It is the promise that we will no longer remain paralyzed by our past, but we will walk fearlessly into all that lies ahead. And if we look closely enough, we might just trace Rahab's footsteps.

Praised throughout Scripture for her fearless faith, she is last mentioned in Hebrews 11:31.

*"By faith the prostitute Rahab, because she welcomed the spies, was not killed with those who were disobedient."*

This is what happens when God intersects our story with grace.

**Astounded,**
*Angela*

(**Excerpt from Session 2:** *Fearless: Ordinary Women of the Bible who Dared to do Extraordinary Things*)

# PIVOT OVER PANIC

*"Do not be anxious about anything, but in every situation, by prayer and petition, with thanksgiving, present your requests to God. And the peace of God, which transcends all understanding, will guard your hearts and your minds in Christ Jesus."*

PHILIPPIANS 4:6-7

Lockdowns and let-downs. N-95 masks and new measures. Social distancing and flattening the curve. As a pandemic swept the globe, 2020 introduced us to unfamiliar terms that soon became household names. Countries implemented unprecedented means to slow the spread of the coronavirus and save lives. Businesses struggled. Families hunkered. Churches changed course. When uncertainty runs rampant, our emotions can become unsettled. Seasons that test our faith tempt us to succumb to fear. However, God gives us tools to pivot instead of panic.

In the book of Philippians, Paul encourages us to keep a heavenly perspective and fight fear with faith. He shares these comforting words in Chapter 4:6-7.

*"Do not be anxious about anything, but in every situation, by prayer and petition, with thanksgiving, present your requests to God. And the peace of God, which transcends all understanding, will guard your hearts and your minds in Christ Jesus."*

I pray we never wage another war with a deadly virus. Yet, we *will* go through times of anguish and doubt. We *will* continue to face moments that take our breath and threaten to take our peace. The enemy wants us to become victims of our circumstances and wallow in worry. He expects us to crumble under soul-splintering conditions. He hopes the strain will be more than we can take. Yet, we are more than conquerors through Christ who gives us strength. We can turn every panic moment into an opportunity to pivot.

## WE CAN EXTRACT THREE TOOLS FROM THIS PASSAGE TO HELP US KNOW HOW TO PIVOT OVER PANIC

**Rehearse the goodness of God instead of the what- ifs.** We can go to God with prayer, petition, and thanksgiving, throughout our day and anytime we feel anxious. Choose to rehearse the goodness of His character instead of all the unknowns that may or may not happen. My piano teacher used to tell me, *"Practice makes permanent,"* and I share that same encouragement with my vocal students. Rehearsing our fears and potential negative outcomes leads to panic. Instead, let's meditate on the goodness of God. The Psalms provide a template for us to trade our refrain of "what-ifs" into worship.

**Reframe worry into prayer.** Worry is a negative form of prayer; it is completely counterproductive. Anxiety and prayer are two formidable opposing forces in the battlefield of our mind. Each day, anxiety and worry face off against gratitude and trust. God gives us the victory as we reframe our fearful thoughts into prayers. God knows and cares about the concerns of our heart. Pray it out in the presence of God and watch worry dissipate. If you're feeling too overwhelmed to pray, reach out and ask others to intercede for you. When we come into agreement with God's Word, heaven responds.

**Release control and receive God's peace.** We receive the promise of peace when we let go and let God. It seems counterintuitive to release control when things around us seem out of control. When panic sets in, we tend to squeeze even tighter when God wants to surrender. When we believe He is in control, we can hand over anything that weighs us down. After the emergency broadcast system interrupts your favorite television program with a blaring signal, these reassuring words fill the screen: *"This was only a test."* Take heart in times of trouble; *this is only a test.* As we trust Him completely, His peace settles our weary hearts and troubled minds.

Many times, we can't control what happens to us. But we can control how we choose to respond to it and what we choose to do with it. Remember we are not left without weapons and tools in our arsenal. When anxiety seeps in and we sense ourselves starting to panic, we can choose to pivot.

**Astounded,**

*Angela*

# TAKE SHELTER

*"Whoever dwells in the shelter of the Most High will rest in the shadow of the Almighty. I will say of the Lord, 'He is my refuge and my fortress, my God, in whom I trust.'"*      PSALM 91:1

*"I'm so overwhelmed,"* my voice cracked with emotion. I trudged through the phone conversation in a fog as the insurance adjuster deemed my car a total loss. Thankfully, my husband graciously picked up where my physical and emotional limitations left off.

Sometimes life pulls out in front of us when we least expect it. In February of 2020, ten seconds shifted every area of my life for months to come. As I made my way through a green light at 45 miles-per-hour, another driver failed to yield. Instinctively, my hand hit the horn and my foot hit the brake. The impact of the collision deployed my air bag, causing a severe concussion and injuries to both hands and wrists. The first few weeks unfolded with doctors' visits and forms galore. X-rays on my wrists proved inconclusive, necessitating an MRI. My injured hand throbbed as they flattened it down inside of a clamp.

My head pounded from a concussion-induced headache. My heart ached from a tumbled mix of unwelcome emotions... disappointment, frustration, fear. *Sigh.*

Tears fell amid whirl and bangs as I laid on my back and stared up at the ominous machine. I questioned why I was on this all-too-familiar road of recovery once again. God comforted my weary mind, body and spirit with the words of Psalm 91:

> *"Whoever dwells in the shelter of the Most High will rest in the shadow of the Almighty. I will say of the Lord, "He is my refuge and my fortress, my God, in whom I trust."*

**Even though life is unpredictable, God's character is unchanging.** He is our Shelter. Our Refuge. Our Fortress. No matter what.

I spent six weeks in a cast to stabilize my right, dominant hand and wrist, followed by invasive, reconstructive surgery on the left. I implemented new strategies from a neurologist and began the process of physical therapy to regain the use of my hand. As I type this last devotional for *"Astounded,"* I am still in the process of recovering.

*"-ing."*

Is it a suffix? Prefix? Whatever it is, I'm struggl-*ing* with "ing." It's dangling on the end of that word, "recovering," in place the much more pleasant, "recovered."

I'm tired of staring at piano keys I can't yet play. I'm drained from depending on others to drive. I'm weary from nagging headaches that slow my pace. Still, life is gradually returning to normal. I am keenly aware that for many who suffer an unexpected impact in life, normal never looks the same. Yet, difficult seasons serve as powerful teachers if we let them. They beckon us to be kinder to ourselves and to others. They ask us to sit with what we're feeling under the Shelter of the Most High. In that sacred space, we surrender our bruised emotions to the God who is our Refuge.

**His Shelter is healing balm to a battered soul.** Psalm 91:14-16 offer 8 reassuring promises to those who love and trust in the Lord:

*"Because he loves me," says the Lord, "I will rescue him; I will protect him, for he acknowledges my name. He will call on me, and I will answer him; I will be with him in trouble, I will deliver him and honor him. With long life I will satisfy him and show him my salvation."*

He rescues us.

He protects us.

He answers us.

He is with us in trouble.

He delivers us.

He honors us.

He satisfies us with long life.

He shows us His salvation.

*He leaves us astounded.*

I add new scars to my collection, ones I can easily see on my hand and wrist. They, like the others, become remembrances, not of simply a dark season, but of the God who is our Refuge. He promises purpose out of pain. In any season, God is our safe place; His presence is always the reprieve we need. Take shelter under His goodness as you keep your eyes peeled for the miracle hidden in everyday moments. Because sometimes, when we least expect it, God breathes on a situation and leaves us astounded.

**Grateful,**

*Angela*

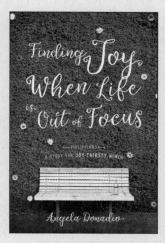

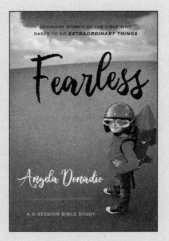